Pembroke Welsh Corgi

2nd Edition

GET MORE!
Visit www.wiley.com/
go/pembrokewelsh
corgi

Debra M. Eldredge, DVM

Howell
Book House™

Howell Book House
Published by Wiley Publishing, Inc., Hoboken, New Jersey

For general information on our other products and services or to obtain technical support please contact our Customer Care Department within the U.S. at (800) 762-2974, outside the U.S. at (317) 572-3993 or fax (317) 572-4002.

Wiley also publishes its books in a variety of electronic formats. Some content that appears in print may not be available in electronic books. For more information about Wiley products, please visit our web site at www.wiley.com.

Library of Congress Cataloging-in-Publication Data:
Eldredge, Debra.
  Pembroke Welsh corgi / Debra Eldredge.—2nd ed.
      p. cm.—(Your happy healthy pet)
  Includes index.
  ISBN 978-0-470-39061-0
  1. Pembroke Welsh corgi. I. Title.
  SF429.P33E43 2009
  636.737—dc22

                                        2008046666

Printed in the United States of America

10 9 8 7 6 5 4 3 2 1

2nd Edition

Book design by Melissa Auciello-Brogan
Cover design by Michael J. Freeland
Illustrations in chapter 9 by Shelley Norris and Karl Brandt
Book production by Wiley Publishing, Inc. Composition Services

About the Author

Debra Eldredge, DVM, is a veterinarian and longtime dog trainer and fancier. She is also an award-winning writer. Her dogs compete in virtually every dog sport and are beloved family companions. She would like to dedicate this book to Flash, her daughter's Pembroke Welsh Corgi, who introduced her to this wonderful breed, and to her beloved shadow, Susan, who came to her as a rehome and stepped right into her heart.

About Howell Book House

Since 1961, Howell Book House has been America's premier publisher of pet books. We're dedicated to companion animals and the people who love them, and our books reflect that commitment. Our stable of authors—training experts, veterinarians, breeders, and other authorities—is second to none. And we've won more Maxwell Awards from the Dog Writers Association of America than any other publisher.

As we head toward the half-century mark, we're more committed than ever to providing new and innovative books, along with the classics our readers have grown to love. From bringing home a new puppy to competing in advanced equestrian events, Howell has the titles that keep animal lovers coming back again and again.

Contents

Shopping List

You'll need to do a bit of stocking up before you bring your new dog or puppy home. Below is a basic list of some must-have supplies. For more detailed information on the selection of each item below, consult chapter 5. For specific guidance on what grooming tools you'll need, review chapter 7.

- [ ] Food dish
- [ ] Water dish
- [ ] Dog food
- [ ] Leash
- [ ] Collar
- [ ] Crate

- [ ] Nail clippers
- [ ] Grooming tools
- [ ] Safe chew toys
- [ ] Toys for play
- [ ] ID tag
- [ ] Treats

There are likely to be a few other items that you're dying to pick up before bringing your dog home. Use the following blanks to note any additional items you'll be shopping for.

- [ ] _____
- [ ] _____
- [ ] _____
- [ ] _____
- [ ] _____
- [ ] _____
- [ ] _____
- [ ] _____
- [ ] _____
- [ ] _____
- [ ] _____
- [ ] _____

Pet Sitter's Guide

We can be reached at (__)_____-_____ Cell phone (__)_____-_____

We will return on _____ (date) at _____ (approximate time)

Dog's Name _____

Breed, Age, and Sex _____

Important Names and Numbers

Vet's Name _____ Phone (__)_____- _____

Address_____

Emergency Vet's Name _____ Phone (__)_____- _____

Address_____

Poison Control _____ (or call vet first)

Other individual (someone the dog knows well and will respond to) to contact in case of emergency or in case the dog is being protective and will not allow the pet sitter in. _____

Care Instructions

In the following three blanks let the sitter know what to feed, how much, and when; when the dog should go out; when to give treats; and when to exercise the dog.

Morning_____

Afternoon _____

Evening _____

Medications needed (dosage and schedule) _____

Any special medical conditions _____

Grooming instructions in detail—Daily: _____

Weekly: _____

My dog's favorite playtime activities, quirks, toys, and other tips _____

Commands my dog knows and will respond to _____

Part I

The World of the Pembroke Welsh Corgi

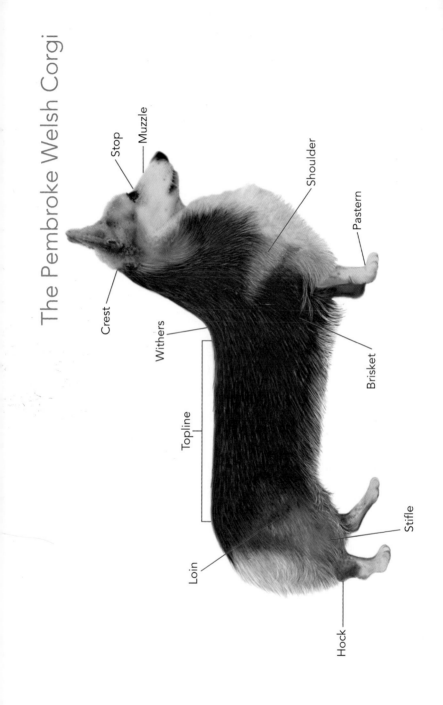

The Pembroke Welsh Corgi

Chapter 1

What Is a Pembroke Welsh Corgi?

The Pembroke Welsh Corgi is a small but tough little dog. He's surprisingly heavy for his size and has sturdy bones and strong muscles. Yet he can move with astonishing speed and great agility. In fact, these dogs are often referred to as "a big dog in a small package."

The Corgi's attributes came in handy on the Welsh farmland, where the breed was developed primarily to herd cattle by nipping at its heels. His job description has changed in modern times, though. He now applies his considerable talents to being a top-notch companion animal.

The American Kennel Club (AKC) places the Pembroke Welsh Corgi in the Herding Group, along with much larger breeds such as the Collie and the German Shepherd Dog. Alongside this company, he competes very successfully at AKC conformation shows and other events.

The Breed Standard

The special characteristics of the Pembroke Welsh Corgi, a herding dog, are clearly described in the breed standard. A good way to learn the basics is to start with this blueprint of the breed. Serious exhibitors and dedicated breeders who strive to produce top-quality Corgis go back to the standard again and again.

What Is a Breed Standard?

A breed standard is a detailed description of the perfect dog of that breed. Breeders use the standard as a guide in their breeding programs, and judges use it to evaluate the dogs in conformation shows. The standard is written by the national breed club, using guidelines established by the registry that recognizes the breed (such as the AKC or UKC).

Usually, the first section of the breed standard gives a brief overview of the breed's history. Then it describes the dog's general appearance and size as an adult. Next is a detailed description of the head and neck, then the back and body, and the front and rear legs. The standard then describes the ideal coat and how the dog should be presented in the show ring. It also lists all acceptable colors, patterns, and markings. Then there's a section on how the dog moves, called *gait*. Finally, there's a general description of the dog's temperament.

Each section also lists characteristics that are considered to be faults or disqualifications in the conformation ring. Superficial faults in appearance are often what distinguish a pet-quality dog from a show- or competition-quality dog. However, some faults affect the way a dog moves or his overall health. And faults in temperament are serious business.

You can read all the AKC breed standards at www.akc.org.

General Appearance

The Pembroke Welsh Corgi is a keen, hardy dog. He possesses an amazing amount of stamina and energy. He is not really a small dog, but rather a short dog. He's got the body of a medium-size dog, but his legs are short. When you look at a Pembroke Welsh Corgi, you see a sturdy dog with enough length of leg to be very agile and fast if he needs to be.

Right away, you should also notice the bright, alert expression from his oval, dark eyes and the very upright ears on his foxy head. Pembroke Welsh Corgis are very smart dogs, interested in the world around them, and of course, in their special humans.

While the average Pembroke Welsh Corgi is sturdy this does not mean blocky or heavy. As a herding dog, the Corgi needs to be fit in mind and body and be ready to take on the task at hand with enthusiasm and endurance. He was designed to be agile enough to avoid the kicks of cattle. His wise approach to life, coupled with a distinct sense of humor, are endearing characteristics.

Size

Ideally, your Pembroke Welsh Corgi will be 10 to 12 inches tall when measured at the withers (the point on the back right at the top of the shoulders). Corgis should not be allowed to get overweight. Most will weigh between 23 and 30 pounds.

The ideal Corgi is longer than he is tall. If you measure from his withers to the base of his tail, he should be about 40 percent longer than his height at the withers.

The breed standard says "moderately long and low" is an essential characteristic of the Pembroke Welsh Corgi. A Corgi who is a good length but too low to the ground because of overly short legs might tire while working in the pasture. A dog with a square outline just doesn't look like a Corgi. A dog who is too tall will lack the sturdiness that was essential for a Welsh herding dog.

In size, as in all Corgi attributes, balance is the key. The dog should be the right weight and size for his look, height, and purpose. No one feature should be exaggerated or emphasized above the others.

Head

Although the Pembroke Corgi has a foxy head, he should not have the narrow, pointed nose and squinty eyes of a fox. A very round head is not desirable either.

The correct amount of stop (the space between the eyes where the skull meets the muzzle) is important.

The Corgi's head can be described as "foxy," but it shouldn't be pointy.

Too abrupt a change, along with a heavy brow, give the dog a blocky look. Too flat a stop leaves the muzzle and forehead flowing together.

Part of the foxy look comes from the erect, medium-size ears, which have a slightly rounded point. The ears are placed on the top of the head and stand up. Corgis move their ears constantly and most expressively. They usually are carried pointing back if the dog is trotting or running, but up and ahead when they are interested in something—which is much of the time. The ears should not be so large that they overwhelm the head, but may appear that way in some young puppies.

The eyes, including the rims, are oval and medium in size. They can be various shades of brown. A dark brown eye, but not truly black, is preferred. Light-colored eyes are considered not as attractive. The eye rims should be black to match the lips and the nose. Sometimes a fine row of black hairs outlines the rims, like mascara.

It is important in dogs like the Pembroke Welsh Corgi with a working heritage that the teeth are correct. Dogs are not allowed to have braces or orthodontic work! In Corgis, the small incisors in front should just overlap, with the top teeth covering the bottom teeth but with no gap between. That way, all of the teeth should align properly and your Corgi can grab things and chew without any problems.

Neck, Topline, and Body

A Pembroke Welsh Corgi should have a moderately long neck. A neck that is too short will make him look stuffy, while a very long neck looks weak.

The topline is the line along back of the dog. In a Corgi, the topline should be level. That is the ideal, though some Corgis may have a slight dip or a roach (upward curve at the rump) on their toplines. This straight back should stay level even when your Corgi is trotting across your yard. At a gallop, it will change as the dog's back flexes.

Pembroke Welsh Corgis have a solid body. Remember, these are medium dogs with short legs. They have a deep chest with plenty of room for their lungs to expand and provide that extra oxygen they need when working.

The loin area on a Corgi is from the end of the rib cage to the top of the hip. While the back may look long, this area should be fairly short, giving your Corgi agility and a short turning radius.

One of the most distinguishing features of the Pembroke Welsh Corgi is his lack of a tail—and thereby hangs a tale! In the early days of the breed, many Pembrokes were born tailless or with short stumps. The natural bobtail may range in length from "barely present" to a couple of inches long. This in no way

The ideal Corgi has a level topline.

hampered their activities. While taillessness is a genetic factor, it is not due to a defective gene.

Over the course of time, breeders selected their stock for other features to improve the breed, and the gene for taillessness ended up being swamped in the gene pool. Many of the puppies born today have long tails. According to the standard, they should be docked as short as possible without being indented. This is done a few days after birth. A tail up to two inches long is allowable if it doesn't spoil the contour of the topline.

In recent years, several countries, including Britain, have banned tail docking in all breeds. Breeders have been working with bloodlines that still carry the gene for a natural bobtail and have produced some fine Corgis without sacrificing other desirable breed qualities. In the United States, docking is still allowed. Nonetheless, a few natural bobtails appear in litters from time to time.

Front Legs

The front legs of the Pembroke Welsh Corgi should not be perfectly straight from the elbows to the ground. Because they have short legs and a deep chest, the forearms (the bone between the wrist and the elbow) have a slight curve so that the wrists are closer together than the elbows. However, this curve should not be exaggerated, and the pasterns (the same area as our wrists) and the feet should be parallel and face forward. Too much of a curve and/or feet that toe out are, unfortunately, common faults that indicate a weakness in the running gear.

The ideal Pembroke Corgi foot is oval, with the two center toes slightly longer than the outer toes. Strong, well-padded feet are a necessity, because they carry the entire weight of the dog and must be tough to cope with rough terrain. To avoid a mishap in the field, dewclaws (the extra toes on the inside of the legs) are usually removed at the time the tail is docked. The nails must be kept short to maintain the tightness of the foot.

Back Legs

Good movement is the result of proper conformation. For the Corgi to move efficiently, his front legs and rear legs must have complementary angulation—the angles of the joints in the legs. The rear produces the driving action and the front legs reach forward. If the angles between the main bones of these two assemblies are widely different, there will be an imbalance. The hind legs have a greater range of flexibility and drive than the front legs, and any imbalance leads to inefficient action.

Good movement is the result of good structure—especially in the rear, which drives a dog's forward motion.

Coat

One of the grandest attributes of the Pembroke Welsh Corgi is his coat. It sheds dirt, doesn't tangle, and protects the dog from temperature extremes. It's also a reasonable length, easy to care for, and water-resistant.

The Corgi has a medium-length double coat, meaning a harder top-coat lies on top of a softer under-coat. The thick undercoat is not noticeable, but adds to the luxurious feel overall. Areas of longer hair pro-vide the attractive full ruff at the neck and fancy pants (also known as pantaloons) on the back legs, as well as the charming "fairy saddle" that is clearly visible at the withers and over the shoulders. The style of his tail-less rear is also enhanced with plush furnishings. Most Corgi coats lie straight, but some will be a bit wavy.

The Corgi's plush coat sometimes comes in a longer variety known as fluffy.

The downside is that the Corgi sheds. During shedding season, your Corgi may lose much of the neck ruff and pantaloons. You will be surprised at how much hair can come out of a small dog!

Some Pembroke Welsh Corgis will be born with a longer, fluffier coat. These are appropriately called *fluffies*, and are simply Corgis with something extra. The fluffy coat is soft, silky, and without the usual hard outer guard hairs that repel burrs and snags. This type of coat may require a bit more daily grooming atten-tion but does tend to shed less. This is a fault for the conformation show ring but does not affect the dog in any other way. Fluffy Corgis are eligible to com-pete in all the performance activities, such as obedience and agility. Some people with pet fluffy Corgis will trim them for easier care.

For Corgis in the show ring, no trimming is allowed, except the whiskers and the foot hair.

Color

Pembroke Welsh Corgis come in a wide variety of colors and shades. Most include flashy areas of white. Reds range from a dark, foxy color to a pale fawn.

Sables are red dogs with black tips on the outer guard hairs, giving the coat a shading of black. Some sables are heavily shaded and some have only a smattering of black, mostly on the shoulders, head, and rump where the tail is set. Often sables show a distinctive cap-like marking over the eyes, giving them an elfish expression.

Tricolors (red or brown, white, and black) come in two basic versions—the red-headed tri and the black-headed tri. The black on a red-headed tri may be a saddle across the back or spread over most of the body. The margins between black and red have a tweedy appearance. The adult head is mostly red or fawn with just a touch of black here and there.

The black-headed tri has a distinct pattern. The skull is black, there is a black stripe on the bridge of the muzzle, the ear tips are black, a black crescent sweeps back on the cheeks, and there are noticeable brown dots over the eyes. Overall, this is a much blacker dog. If there were no white markings, the legs would be brown and there would even be black dots on top of the toes and brown under the tail.

In Corgis, white usually breaks up the total pattern. The standard requires some red or tan, however pale, to be present, because pure black and white is not allowed.

Well-placed white markings dress up the basic coloring. Almost all Pembroke Welsh Corgis have white socks and at least a splash of white on the chest. Some shine with full white collars. On others, a blaze or snippet on the muzzle looks attractive. There is endless variation, and no two Corgis ever seem to be exactly the same. This is much more fun than the solid colors of many other breeds, and helps to identify individuals.

As with the coat texture, the wrong amount or incorrect placement of the white can be considered a fault for the show ring. *Mismark*s are dogs with any white on the back between the withers and tail, on the sides between the elbows and the back of the hindquarters, or above an imaginary horizontal line drawn from the elbow to the stifle, or on the ears. *Whitelies* have a white body with red or dark markings, sometimes big spots, and are rare. While Pembroke Welsh Corgis with color faults are not good show ring prospects, they are still wonderful family companions.

Gait

Gait is the way a dog moves. A Corgi with correct skeletal proportions and firm muscles will achieve the breed's purposeful, ground-covering gait. Since Pembroke Welsh Corgis were originally bred as herding dogs, their movement must be free, easy, and agile, with stamina to work for long periods.

Good movement is essential to a breed like the Corgi, which was developed to herd livestock all day.

It is a joy to behold a well-balanced Corgi trotting purposefully along on a loose leash. The ears are laid back, the head is held fairly low, the topline is level, and those short legs work with strength and efficiency. Good movement looks effortless. He could go on all day without tiring.

Temperament

Although the section on temperament in the breed standard is short, Corgi enthusiasts know how their dogs should act. Emotional stability, self-confidence, and enthusiasm for life are of prime importance. Curiosity, intelligence, inventiveness, humor, sensitivity, trainability, loyalty, and affection are all typical of a Corgi's wonderful mind.

As with the physical attributes of the dog, the key is balance. An ideal Pembroke Welsh Corgi has an all-encompassing, overall balance. He should be enthusiastic but controllable, able to make you laugh and cuddle on your lap, but at the same time guard his family with a sharp bark when needed. Chapter 3 will expand on the various aspects of the Corgi personality.

Chapter 2

The History of Welsh Corgis

A charming legend has been passed down through the generations regarding the Corgi's history. Children playing in the woods found two puppies with foxy faces and short legs and brought them home. The grownups said they were gifts from the fairies, who used them as fairy steeds to draw their carriages. When the children's dogs got older, they were helpful with many tasks on the farm and with the livestock, just as Corgis are today. As proof of their connection to the spirit world, Pembroke Corgis still carry the marks of the fairy saddle on their backs. (You will also see fairies included in many pieces of Pembroke Welsh Corgi artwork.)

Separate Histories

The first historical mention of what may have been a Corgi was in the Laws of Hvwel Dda, king of South Wales, codified around the year 920. A "herds-man's cur" (or dog) was differentiated from a "house cur" and a "watch cur." Some breed historians believe the Corgi was the only type of herding dog established in Wales until the 1800s, and the Laws might authenticate the Corgi's existence in the tenth century. However, the reference could have been to any sort of dog the farmer used for herding, because in those days most dogs had to have many talents to earn their keep.

A better developed, if not actually substantiated, theory was outlined by W. Lloyd-Thomas in a series of articles first published in 1935 in the magazine

Corgis have a very long history as herding dogs in Wales. They move larger animals by nipping at their heels.

Pure-Bred Dogs American Kennel Gazette. He said the Pembroke and the Cardigan Welsh Corgi stem from entirely different stock. Pembrokes descend from northern spitz-type dogs (such as the Siberian Husky) with characteristic prick ears, pointed muzzle, thick coat, and a tail that curls over the back. Over the years, though, selection for other traits also apparently selected for the tailless gene.

The ancestors of the Pembroke arrived in Wales with the Flemish weavers around 1107. Eventually, according to Lloyd-Thomas, the drop-eared "original" Corgi in Cardiganshire was refined by interbreeding with other varieties of herding dogs. This took place after 1875—a year that marks the change from pasturing cattle on common land to the use of property boundaries.

The short build of the Corgis allowed them to nip at the heels of cattle, then quickly duck to avoid getting injured from a swift kick. Their skill at chasing neighboring farmers' cows out of a favored grazing area in the common land was to be replaced by herding abilities of other breeds aimed at rounding up and confining cattle.

Viking Dogs

A second theory was offered by another student of both breeds, Clifford Hubbard. He suggested that the Vikings from Norway brought spitz-type dogs with them on their forays to Wales in the ninth and tenth centuries. It is true that a Nordic breed, the Vallhund, looks very much like a grayish, long-legged Corgi. If the Vallhund was crossed with native dogs in south Wales, the result might have been similar to the Pembroke, especially if there was added influence from Flemish dogs—possibly early Schipperkes or Pomeranians.

The flaw in this theory is that modern Vallhunds come from Sweden, not Norway, and they are the wrong color. But they can have natural bobtails, which seems to be evidence of a connection between them and the Pembroke.

The most recent theory has been put forward by Iris Coombe, a researcher on the herding breeds. In a book published in 1987, *Herding Dogs: Their Origins and Development in Britain,* she discusses the eighth-century Scandinavian people who regularly visited the seacoast of western Britain to procure birds, eggs, and feathers from the heavily populated rookeries. They probably brought with them dogs similar to Lundehunds, another spitz-type breed that was particularly adept at working through the rocky terrain in quest of birds.

Lundehunds, or Puffin Dogs, are an ancient and pure Celtic breed that resembles Pembroke Corgis, except they have long legs. What is more, they are the same color.

The feather and fowl trade persisted in later centuries. Coombe says Pembroke Corgis were used to round up and pen poultry and even to drive flocks of large birds to market. Many modern-day Corgis work ducks in herding trials.

Nobody is really sure what the word "Corgi" means. It might be as simple as "little dog."

What's a Corgi?

The origins of the name *Corgi* are even less clear than the breed's history. Again, breed historians have various explanations. Some think it's derived from the Welsh word *cur,* meaning "to watch over." Others credit the Celts, whose word for "dog" was *corgi.* At the time of the Norman Conquest of Britain (1066 to 1072) this was corrupted to *curgi* or *cur,* meaning any small mutt. In Wales, the name came to include any small cattle dog.

Other scholars hunted through ancient Welsh writings to find *corgi* or *korgi* used to mean to "cur" or "cur dog." Thus, the Welsh herdsman's cur would be the Welsh Corgi.

Another possibility is that *cor* is Welsh for "dwarf" and *gi* is a word for "dog." In any case, the breed was known mostly as Welsh Curs well into the nineteenth century. Although *corgwyn* is the Welsh plural of "corgi," the correct spelling for more than one is *Corgis* (no E).

Coming off the Farm

During the later part of the 1800s, Corgis were very popular on Pembrokeshire farms. They began to be exhibited at local agricultural shows under the classification Cwn Sodli ("heeling dogs"), Heelers, and Curs.

In 1925, Corgis first appeared at a show under the rules of The Kennel Club in Britain. Pembrokes and Cardigans were shown together. In December 1925, the Corgi Club was founded in Carmarthen, Pembrokeshire. Naturally, the local members favored the Pembroke breed, so a year later a club for Cardigan enthusiasts was created. Both are still in existence.

Each group worked hard to standardize the appearance and type of its breed through careful selective breeding. The first standard for Corgis (both Pembroke and Cardigan) was drawn up in 1925. It was not long before these stylish little dogs began to attract attention. They were officially recognized by the Kennel Club in 1928, but both were lumped together under the heading Welsh Corgis.

Pembrokes and Cardigans

At one point, there were some hard feelings between the supporters of each breed and gray areas as to which was which. One notable litter produced both a Pembroke and a Cardigan champion. Finally, in 1934, the Kennel Club officially separated the breeds.

The two breeds are now markedly different in appearance and, to a certain extent, in temperament. Cardigans are now heavier and longer in body. They have long tails, which are carried low or level. The ears are larger and carried a bit more to the side. Also, the legs are not as straight. Pembrokes can be thought of as the "souped up" version of Corgis. They are more athletic, slightly shorter in body and straighter of leg. The ears are a bit smaller and the expression more foxy. They tend to be more lively and active, as well.

Becoming Royalty

The Pembroke Welsh Corgi was extremely fortunate to come to the attention of Thelma Gray, an Englishwoman and owner of Rozavel Kennels. She applied her considerable talent and amazing energy to developing and promoting the breed.

For a long time, her Ch. (the abbreviation for champion) Rozavel Red Dragon, born in 1932, was the top-producing British sire of all time, with thirteen champions to his credit.

It was from Gray that the Duke of York, later King George VI, bought a Corgi puppy in 1933 for his two daughters, Elizabeth and Margaret Rose. Since then, the British royal family has enjoyed a steady line of Corgis that have given them companionship and support through the rigors of royal life. Queen Elizabeth II tends to her Corgis herself and even personally selects the sires of litters that are bred in her kennel. After seventy-five years, she certainly is the epitome of breed loyalty!

Needless to say, royal interest in the Pembroke Welsh Corgi had quite an effect on the breed's popularity. Long gone are the days of the Corgi's obscurity on the farms of southern Wales. Pembrokes span the globe and are especially numerous in several nations of the British Commonwealth, particularly Australia and New Zealand.

The Trip to America

While on a trip to London in 1933, Mrs. Lewis Roesler (later Mrs. Edward Renner) chanced upon a show-bound red and white Pembroke named Little Madam in Paddington Station. It was love at first sight, and she bought the dog

As a breed, Corgis have flourished in North America, and there are many fine kennels producing top dogs.

What Is the AKC?

The American Kennel Club (AKC) is the oldest and largest pure-bred dog registry in the United States. Its main function is to record the pedigrees of dogs of the breeds it recognizes. While AKC registration papers are a guarantee that a dog is pure-bred, they are absolutely not a guarantee of the quality of the dog—as the AKC itself will tell you.

The AKC makes the rules for all the canine sporting events it sanctions and approves judges for those events. It is also involved in various public education programs and legislative efforts regarding dog ownership. The AKC has also helped establish a foundation to study canine health issues and a program to register microchip numbers for companion animal owners. The AKC has no individual members—its members are national and local breed clubs and clubs dedicated to various competitive sports.

on the spot. In the spring of 1934, Little Madam and a young dog from a Corgi kennel in Wales returned to Mrs. Roesler's famous Merriedip Old English Sheepdog Kennels in Massachusetts and became the first Pembroke Welsh Corgis to set foot in America. That same year, they became the first Pembrokes registered with the American Kennel Club. Little Madam later earned her AKC championship.

In February 1936, during the Westminster Kennel Club Dog Show in New York City, the Pembroke Welsh Corgi Club of America (PWCCA) held its first meeting. The PWCCA is the parent club of the breed and is in charge of developing and maintaining the breed standard. The PWCCA has affiliated member clubs throughout the country, and its annual national specialty show (a dog show limited just to Pembroke Welsh Corgis who compete for national honors) attracts hundreds of the nation's top Corgis for keen competition.

Pembrokes Today

During the years before World War II, many excellent kennels were established on both sides of the Atlantic. While British-bred Corgis will always be admired and exported to other countries for their special heritage, many kennels world-wide now breed top-notch Corgis.

The Pembroke Welsh Corgi in America has flourished over the past eight decades. Kennels throughout the United States are producing dogs of lovely quality. British imports are introduced from time to time, and American Corgis have been exported to other countries to widen their gene pools.

Purebred dogs have become popular family companions over recent years. Many families want to add a companion of known size and temperament. The Pembroke Welsh Corgi currently ranks twenty-second in AKC registrations. They are certainly not rare, but conscientious breeders don't want them to become trendy throwaway pets.

Claims to Fame

In addition to Queen Elizabeth, who is arguably the most famous Corgi owner of all, other noteworthy individuals have surrounded themselves with these special dogs. The well-known artist and illustrator Tasha Tudor invariably includes sketches of her beloved family of Corgis in her exquisite drawings. Tudor lives in a quaint New England farmhouse surrounded by beautiful gardens and assorted ducks, geese, goats, and cats, all of which are depicted in charming detail in her numerous books and greeting cards. Caleb, a handsome red and white Corgi, is the hero of two fanciful books by Tudor, *Corgiville Fair* and *The Great Corgiville Kidnapping*.

A few of the luminaries who owned Pembrokes are the opera singer Beverly Sills, actress Ava Gardner (who was given her last Corgi by Frank Sinatra, her husband at the time), Gregory Peck, France's General Charles de Gaulle, and Olympic gold-medal diver Greg Louganis.

A dog who has been successful in the show ring is Ch. Just Enuff of The Real Thing (known as Fizz), co-owned by Coca-Cola chairman, Roberto C. Goizueta.

Agile Corgi

Kenneth Boyd's Pembroke Welsh Corgi, Becky (officially known as Tafarnwr Green Woods Bechen), set the agility world on fire when she won the national championships for her height divisions for the NADAC (North American Dog Agility Council), AKC (American Kennel Club), and USDAA (United States Dog Agility Association) all in one year.

Many creative people, from Stephen King to Beverly Sills, have been inspired by these loyal, spunky little dogs.

The character Ein from the anime series *Cowboy Bebop* is a genius Pembroke Welsh Corgi. Nintendogs includes a puppy Pembroke Welsh Corgi.

Novelist Stephen King used his Corgi Marlowe as the basis for the character Oy in the Dark Tower series. Novelist Anne Tyler owned a Pembroke, too. Murder mystery fans will love the books of Rita Mae Brown, which feature a wonderful Pembroke Welsh Corgi named Tucker. There is even a movie of one of the books, called *Murder She Purred*. Emily Carmichael has a delightful series of light romances that feature a Corgi as well.

Many Corgis have been trained as service dogs for people with hearing disabilities. Others work as therapy dogs visiting schools and nursing homes. In 2007, the AKC honored Pembroke Welsh Corgi Penni and her handler, Florence Scarinci, as the top Therapy Dog in their Awards for Canine Excellence. Penni visits nursing homes, a school for the deaf, and a school for neglected boys, and also works in a program where children read to dogs to improve their reading skills. That's a lot of love coming from one small dog!

Chapter 3

Why Choose a Pembroke Welsh Corgi?

There are many great reasons for choosing a Pembroke Welsh Corgi to be a member of your family. One of the biggest reasons is the wonderful mind these dogs possess. The mind of the Pembroke Welsh Corgi is special—to know it is to love the breed. To ignore it means you are missing out on the opportunity for a truly wonderful relationship with your dog. And, to be perfectly honest, you ignore that mind at your own peril. An energetic, intelligent dog with no direction and nothing to do is trouble waiting to happen.

It doesn't take more than a moment to realize that your Corgi is one smart little fellow. Regardless of age, the alert expression and awareness of his surroundings are immediately obvious. He easily gets his point across with a meaningful glance and body or ear language.

It's not hard to learn how to "read" members of the breed, and learning to "think dog" is essential to enjoying a Corgi's world. Meanwhile, of course, your Corgi is learning to "read human!"

Energy and Activity

Corgis need to expend energy and thrive in a household with an active lifestyle. There aren't any cattle to chase in the average American backyard, so the Corgi must now devote his ample energies to other activities. But a Corgi loves to be busy exercising or playing. He is always ready for a game of fetch, dashing out and returning to your feet with the prize stuffed in his mouth.

Corgis also enjoy long hikes (snuffling along the way), romps on the beach or at the lake, and learning tricks. If you were hoping for a couch potato companion, realize that most Corgis do *not* fit that description—or at least not until they reach senior citizen status. A few Corgis will be simple "love bugs," but most have places to go and things to do.

Fun, Games, and, of Course, Rest

It's great fun to play "find the ball" under the fall leaves or "where-did-that-yellow-thing-go-in-all-this-cold-white-stuff?" in the winter. Most every Corgi can be an avid ballplayer when given the chance. It is a super way to give your dog the daily exercise he needs when your schedule does not allow time for a long walk.

Although he loves to play, the Corgi is not a hyperactive dog who constantly demands more and more action. He will settle down quietly for a short snooze or peacefully pursue the merits of a chew toy or bone. He is a sensible, comfortable companion.

Corgis are active, busy little dogs. But with a little creativity, you can find ways to keep them busy in an apartment.

Teenage Corgis, from about six to eighteen months of age, may not have a very good "off switch." At this age, they may need extra exercise and be less likely to lie down quietly in the evening. Be prepared for some long evening hikes, and have plenty of good chew items on hand. (Chapter 5 addresses appropriate items for chewing.)

Although they would prefer having a yard, many Corgis adjust happily to apartments and life on a leash. It is the quality of the time he gets that counts—although daily exercise is necessary for his physical and mental well-being.

Corgi Character

Corgis are curious. Introduce any new item and your dog will be on the spot evaluating with sniffing nose, bristling whiskers, and probing paw. Then he will proceed appropriately: Check out the comfort level and size of the new dog bed, bark at the box turtle, avoid the artichoke. He always has to know what's going on. It is hard to sneak anything past a Corgi.

The Corgi is also inventive. To avoid boredom, he will play with his toys in an amusing and creative way. More than one Corgi has figured out that dropping a ball down the stairs is the answer when no one is around to throw it. One little guy perfected his ability to maneuver a soccer ball around the yard for half an hour at a time without ever losing control of it. I know of one Corgi who invented "scooter bone," whereby he stepped on and pushed a bone along with one front paw and barked gleefully at the moving object. The same Corgi used to pounce on the dry dirt with his paws together and squirt up puffs of dust that he practiced biting just for the fun of it!

Corgis enjoy cold weather and love to play in the snow. They may dig into it, run along with their nose in the snow, or roll around making Corgi versions of snow angels. They are nice and warm with their double coats and do not need sweaters or jackets. If the snow is very deep and soft, your Corgi may need a path dug for him to run about safely.

Corgis observe their owners closely. If you are about to go out, even if you don't tell him that he is not going to accompany you, he will amble over to his favorite resting spot and flop down. He may indeed have read your mind, or perhaps he figured out that you always comb your hair in front of a certain mirror just before you leave on a non-doggy excursion. He knows you very well.

Some dogs take charge when squabbling siblings need to be separated. They will snuggle up to a teary tot or herd the child away from potential danger. A

The Dog's Senses

The dog's eyes are designed so that he can see well in relative darkness, has excellent peripheral vision, and is very good at tracking moving objects—all skills that are important to a carnivore. Dogs also have good depth perception. Those advantages come at a price, though: Dogs are nearsighted and are slow to change the focus of their vision. It's a myth that dogs are color-blind. However, while they can see some (but not all) colors, their eyes were designed to most clearly perceive subtle shades of gray—an advantage when they are hunting in low light.

Dogs have about six times fewer taste buds on their tongue than humans do. They can taste sweet, sour, bitter, and salty flavors, but with so few taste buds it's likely that their sense of taste is not very refined.

A dog's ears can swivel independently, like radar dishes, to pick up sounds and pinpoint their location. Dogs can locate a sound in $\frac{6}{100}$ of a second and hear sound four times farther away than we can (which is why there is no reason to yell at your dog). They can also hear sounds at far higher pitches than we can.

In their first few days of life, puppies primarily use their sense of touch to navigate their world. Whiskers on the face, above the eyes, and below the jaws are sensitive enough to detect changes in airflow. Dogs also have touch-sensitive nerve endings all over their bodies, including on their paws.

Smell may be a dog's most remarkable sense. Dogs have about 220 million scent receptors in their nose, compared to about 5 million in humans, and a large part of the canine brain is devoted to interpreting scent. Not only can dogs smell scents that are very faint, but they can also accurately distinguish between those scents. In other words, when you smell a pot of spaghetti sauce cooking, your dog probably smells tomatoes and onions and garlic and oregano and whatever else is in the pot.

Corgi will run and bark in a call for help. One Corgi repeatedly pressed himself against his fallen friend, who lived alone, in an effort to boost her to her feet.

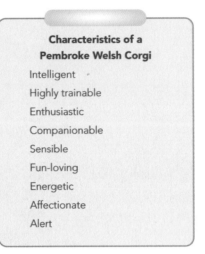

Characteristics of a Pembroke Welsh Corgi

Intelligent

Highly trainable

Enthusiastic

Companionable

Sensible

Fun-loving

Energetic

Affectionate

Alert

Concern may extend to other pets as well. A young Corgi alerted his owner that his elderly deaf and blind canine companion had wandered out of the safety of the garden. Another dog rushed to protect "his" cat from the over-exuberant advances of a passing puppy. Back on the Welsh farms, the Corgi was counted upon to use his brains for the welfare of the other animals.

Your Corgi will take his role as a family member very seriously. While Corgis tend to attach most strongly to one person, they are wonderful family dogs and will do their best to love everyone. Without being cloying, the Corgi gives honest affection and loves to receive it. He is always right there, happy to be noticed, ready to comfort when spirits are low, in sync with every mood. Rapport between the Corgi and his person is intense, which is why the breed can do exceptionally well in performance events such as obedience and agility.

A breed that cares this much is also going to be quite sensitive. Hardy as they are, Corgis do not do well with any form of harsh treatment. Should the need arise to reprimand him, a firm "no" and a stern look are usually enough. A Corgi has a tremendous desire to please. With kind treatment and respect, this keenly intelligent dog can be trained to do almost anything. He is quick to learn, so take the opportunity to teach him positive things.

Follow the Leader

If the Corgi has a downside, it stems from the fact that he is super-smart and has a strong sense of his own being. A willful chap can and sometimes does get the upper paw on an owner who cannot stay one pace ahead of him. A Corgi needs a leader he respects, or he might assume the position himself.

As cute as his antics may he, he must learn at once what is appropriate and who is boss. A Corgi is not for someone who is unwilling to accept this challenge. These dogs were bred to boss around cattle. This is a breed with moxie—an amazing amount for the size of the dog. To the tougher individuals, a mere human is not much of a challenge. If you start right from puppyhood with firm but gentle training to establish what is and what isn't acceptable behavior, your Corgi will respect and love you. Otherwise, your Corgi may decide to take over.

Barking and Strangers

The Corgi has always been valued as a watchdog. His acute hearing alerts him to unusual sounds, and his big dog bark means business when something is amiss. The Corgi has a variety of barks to suit any occasion, but he does not yap or carry on incessantly. When announcing the arrival of a visitor, he will stop barking as soon as he knows the person is welcome. Some Corgis are reserved with strangers, but once they have been introduced, most happily greet a new friend.

If a Corgi is left alone for long periods or not given enough exercise and attention, he may start to bark simply to amuse himself. Corgis love to look out windows, even if it requires getting up on a chair or a couch to do so. From there, he can observe the neighborhood, perhaps barking at squirrels coming into his yard or even at blowing leaves.

Corgis are curious and inventive and definitely have a sense of humor.

Corgis and Other Animals

On the Welsh farms, the Pembroke Corgi naturally involved himself with all kinds of domestic animals. Today, the breed is a favorite of equestrians across the country. Corgis seem to have a special, calming way around the horses, neither fearing nor annoying them.

Cats and Corgis can be a good combination, too. Animals who grow up together often form true friendships. The same is true of small pets such as rabbits and guinea pigs. Corgis did work as ratters on their farms, though, and many retain hunting instincts. They need to learn which animals are not prey. Although generalizations can be made, ultimately it depends on the individual Corgi. If your Corgi has strong hunting instincts, he should not be left alone with your pocket pets.

Corgis and Other Corgis

Corgis are such charming dogs that owning one often leads to acquiring another. This is fine. In fact, two Corgis are much more than the sum of one and one. Watching their dog-to-dog antics will bring a smile to any face. In addition, two are seldom more trouble to care for than one. However, one Corgi of each sex is by far the best combination. While many well-organized multi-Corgi

Corgis can be bossy dogs. Early training will help head that off.

Cats and Corgis can be friends, especially if they grow up together.

households exist harmoniously, these dogs frequently do not get along as well with others of the same sex.

Proper socialization from puppyhood teaches them good behavior in a crowd of other dogs and is a must. Undisciplined dogs can be aggressive to other canines.

If you have multiple Corgis, is it crucial to be sure that you spend private time with each dog individually. Otherwise, the dogs may bond to one another and you will be the "outsider." It is usually not a good idea to bring home littermates. Those puppies will tend even more to bond to one another.

Corgis and Kids

And how will your dog get along with children? A Corgi who has been treated with kindness and respect by children will respond with obvious enjoyment, loyalty, and tolerance. He will love kids. However, he will not tolerate mean or hurtful behavior and will leave the scene or even make his point clear in a less gracious manner. It is essential that an adult insist on gentleness toward the dog from both their own children and other young folks.

It should be noted that the Corgi's innate herding instinct is often expressed by nipping at flying heels. This is not acceptable. It may be difficult to train the dog out of this behavior, but it's definitely necessary. You need to clearly point out to your Corgi that this is not acceptable behavior. If you are consistent in your reminders and act the minute you see this behavior start, you will have better success. Training the children not to encourage the dog's inclination is equally important.

The Size Factor

Many families today live in apartments or neighborhoods with small yards. A Corgi can be the perfect canine fit because he's relatively small and doesn't take up the entire living room rug or hog the whole couch.

A well-behaved Corgi will ride well in the car in his crate or with a doggie seatbelt. He won't require his own row of seats, but happily curls up in the seating space of one human. He may even be able to fly in an airplane under the seat in a cloth traveling bag.

Many hotels that refuse to accept large dogs will allow Corgis to stay because they are small. And a Corgi easily fits into a crowded elevator where a Great Dane would not.

Corgis get along well with children as long as there is mutual respect. No matter how gentle the kid or the dog, though, you should always supervise dogs and young children.

With a Corgi you're getting an energetic, sturdy, and willing partner.

A Lot of Dog in a Small Package

Despite the economies of size, you are still getting a lot of dog with a Corgi. This is a dog who will be able to take a morning jog with you, play with a flying disc at the park, or swim at the lake with you. Corgis are energetic and athletic and can participate in virtually any dog sport you might want to try.

While their size might not put off a determined burglar, the loud bark and wild charge will deter most unwanted company.

A Corgi should not be left alone with small children, but they are a good size for a child's first dog. They are sturdy enough to handle some roughhousing but small enough that even the average 7-year-old can control them. They are smart and learn tricks quickly—often better than their formal obedience exercises.

Corgis can easily go on camping trips and even carry their own appropriate-size backpack. They fit into a tent or a canoe easily without taking up a large amount of space. A good Corgi motto would be "Corgis on the go, anywhere, any time!"

Chapter 4

Choosing Your Very Own Corgi

Our two Pembroke Welsh Corgis came to us in slightly different ways. My daughter, Kate, had wanted a Corgi since she was 5 years old. I told her she had to wait until she was 7, but in the meantime she could learn about them and prove her ability to care for a dog by taking care of her stuffed dog. So for two years we took a stuffed toy dog virtually everywhere we went.

When it was time to look for a puppy, I contacted Corgi people I knew—people who breed, show, and compete in canine sports with their dogs—and asked for breeder recommendations. Because we participate in many sports with our dogs, and knowing that this puppy was to be the responsibility of a child, we needed just the right puppy. We brought Flash home on Valentine's Day in 1998 when she was 10 weeks old.

Kate lost some sleep housetraining her puppy and learned to be careful about where she kept her toys. But Flash is still a wonderful member of our family at over 10 years of age.

Susan is Flash's dam (mother). When Susan was 8 years old, her breeder went through a divorce and had to rehome many of her dogs. We took in Susan. She was well trained, wonderfully socialized, and fit right into our family. She died at 15, after sharing seven wonderful years with us.

There are a number of places to find the perfect Corgi for your family. A Corgi should *not* be an impulse purchase! You need to do your research ahead of time so you can find the best possible family member.

Reputable Breeders

It is wise to purchase your new Corgi pup from a reputable breeder. The pup will be accustomed to a crate, have started housetraining, and be well socialized to a variety of people. From her littermates and dam, she will have learned proper "dog respect." From growing up in clean surroundings, she will be well on the way to keeping herself and her area clean. You will also have the wonderful resource of a knowledgeable breeder to call upon for the life of your dog.

You can find a reputable breeder through the AKC web site (www.akc.org) or the Pembroke Welsh Corgi Club of America site (www.pwcca.org). If there are dog shows nearby, go and watch the Pembroke Welsh Corgi judging. (You can find dog show listings at www.akc.org and www.infodog.com.) At the show, wait until the breed judging is over to approach the Corgi handlers. Before judging they will be busy grooming and preparing their Corgis for the ring.

You may find that you click with a certain breeder and her dogs. Be prepared to wait for a puppy. Most reputable breeders do not have puppies available all the time. It is definitely worth waiting to get the ideal puppy.

A reputable breeder will allow you to meet the dam and often the sire (father) of the litter (though the sire may live far away). They will also ask you many questions. Do not be put off if the breeder asks you to fill out a questionnaire

Reputable breeders start their puppies off right, so you are able to get the best possible companion.

and provide references. Their goal is to make the best possible match for family and puppy. Breeders want their dogs to live in loving, forever homes.

By meeting the other Corgis who may live at the breeder's home, you can judge the temperament of the dogs. You can also see that your puppy grew up in a clean atmosphere and was provided with plenty of socialization and stimulation.

You need to ask the breeder about any health clearances they have for the parents, what sort of activity level you should expect, and what commitments you need to make about this puppy.

Top-notch breeders will not send their puppies to new homes before 8 to 10, or even 12 weeks of age. They want the puppies through any fear periods in their development. Fear periods are short times during puppy development when pups are very sensitive to new or scary events. Most puppies handle these times best if they still have the mental support of their dam and littermates. They also want to be sure their puppies are adequately socialized with people and other dogs and their environment.

Newspaper Ads

You will need to do extra homework to evaluate the background of a puppy advertised this way. Be sure to see the dam and to look at where the puppies

Be sure to look at where the puppies are being raised before you make a purchase.

The Rule of Sevens

Reputable breeders follow the Rule of Sevens when socializing their puppies. The Rule of Sevens was devised by Pat Schaap, a Shetland Sheepdog breeder. She felt that early exposures to a wide variety of things is important for solid temperaments. Under her program, breeders have a lot of responsibility. Ideally, by the time puppies are 7 weeks old, they should be on seven types of footing and in seven different locations. They should be exposed to seven new people and seven new objects. They should eat out of seven different types of food containers and be fed in seven different spots. They should also face seven different puppy challenges. This might be going up a small step, racing through a play tunnel, or something similar. These are minimums, of course, and many breeders do much more.

were raised. If a local breeder is not willing to let you come over, all sorts of alarms should go off in your head.

Those warnings should go off even louder if you see an ad or a sign for "Corgi puppies—free to good home." These people are simply looking get rid of dogs they no longer want and probably put very little time, care, and attention into. Remember, you get what you pay for!

Health Clearances

A reputable breeder should show you health clearances for a puppy's sire and dam. These are certificates that show the dogs have been tested for and certified clear of certain inherited health problems.

- The Orthopedic Foundation for Animals (OFA) currently keeps a database for many hereditary problems, not just orthopedic ones.
- The Pennsylvania Hip Improvement Plan (PennHIP) is the hip certification program developed and run by the University of Pennsylvania. Specifically, it certifies dogs to be free of hip dysplasia.
- The Canine Eye Registry Foundation (CERF) is organized through Purdue University. It certifies dogs to be free of heritable eye disease.

- The Canine Health Information Center (CHIC) is a new health registry. Each breed club designates which health clearances they feel breeding dogs should have. If a dog has had all the testing done for her breed, that dog is given a CHIC number.

At a minimum, both the sire and the dam should have hip clearances from OFA or PennHIP and eye clearances from CERF, and the breeder should show you copies of the certificates.

The Paperwork

Many breeders will have a sales contract for their puppies. This may state that your puppy must be spayed or neutered by a certain age, or that if you are ever unable to keep your Corgi, she must be returned to the breeder. Most contracts also have some kind of health guarantee as well.

A reputable breeder will have the puppy's AKC registration papers ready to go at the same time the puppy is. The breeder will also provide you with a pedigree and information on what health care your pup has already been given, such as vaccinations and any dewormings, plus a sample of your pup's diet.

Puppies have individual personalities. Try to pick the pup who will best fit in with your family.

Which Pup for Me?

When choosing your pup, look for one who is outgoing but not too rowdy. You don't want the shy pup in the corner, but you don't want the litter bully, either. Very often the breeder will tell you which puppy would be the best match for your family based on temperament testing and her observations.

This is where any questionnaire you filled out and conversations you had with the breeder will be a great help. The breeder needs to know if your Corgi is to be simply a family companion or if you also want to show her in conformation or performance. A white spot in the wrong area could mean no show ring career, but that puppy would still be a fabulous agility, obedience, or pet prospect. A "fluffy" is not a conformation show prospect but can be a fun-loving family member and performance prospect. Plus, they are cute!

Temperament Testing

There are a number of puppy temperament tests that can help you decide which puppy is right for you. They all consist of little exercises, with a way to score them and a chart that interprets what the scores mean.

The little exercises are an attempt to figure out the basic personality of the puppy. This is a "snapshot," though—just one moment in time. While it may predict a puppy's future behavior quite well, if the puppy is tired or not feeling well on that day, the test will not be an accurate reflection of her personality. Also, environmental factors such as socialization and training can greatly influence a Corgi's personality. Still, the puppy tests can be a starting place for finding the right Corgi for you.

It is generally recommended to do the temperament testing at 49 days of age. At this age, the pups are neurologically grown up but haven't been affected by a great deal of learning.

To do the tests, the puppies should be taken to a place they have not been before. The tester should be someone who does not know them but who is knowledgeable about dogs and dog behavior. Someone who is familiar with the breed is ideal. If possible, a third person will help by scoring the individual tests. Puppies are tested one at a time.

The ideal family Corgi will score in the "middle of the road" range for most tests. You want a pup who wants to be with and work with people but who is not overly sensitive or reactive to sights, sounds, and touch.

> **TIP**
>
> An excellent puppy temperament test was developed by legendary dog trainers Wendy and Jack Volhard. You can find it at www.volhard.com/pages/pat.php.

Very few pups will score totally in the middle range, but you want a pup with a majority of those middle scores.

While puppy testing can provide valuable information, the breeder's input is equally or even more important. Your Corgi's breeder will have watched over the litter carefully from the minute the pups were born. They will have observed the playing and mini dominance fights among the littermates. They will have a very good idea of how each pup will develop.

Adding an Adult Corgi

You may decide that a puppy is not the best choice for your family. A wonderful alternative can be to take in a Corgi from a breed rescue group. That's a group dedicated to finding Corgis in need, such as those turned in to shelters by families that are moving or in economic straits. The Corgis are then taken out of the shelters and placed in foster homes until a "forever" home can be found. Rescue groups generally spay or neuter their Corgis and do basic health care and screening before placing their charges. Most rescue groups place their Corgis in foster homes with experienced Corgi people who can evaluate the dog for any behavior or temperament problems.

> **TIP**
>
> At all times, remember that your goal should be to find the perfect Corgi for your family. Think realistically about what you want in your new canine family member. Be clear when you speak to rescue people or breeders about how you expect to fit this wonderful puppy or dog into your life.

The Corgis looking for new homes through rescue and well-run shelters will also have had behavior and temperament screening. With an adult Corgi, you have a very good idea of the dog's temperament. And having an adult is much easier in terms of things like chewing and housetraining.

Some of the Corgis who end up in rescue may have behavior problems or "baggage" from their earlier life. The foster family who has kept the Corgi can enlighten you about any problems. They may have determined that a certain Corgi would not do well in a home with any cats or toddlers. That same Corgi might be perfect for a family with teenagers, though. At least this way, you know ahead of time what difficulties you may face.

An adult dog can be a great addition to your family.

Adult Dogs from Shelters

Some Corgis may be found at shelters or humane societies. Corgis who end up in shelters might be barkers or diggers, or they might simply have been dropped off by families that no longer want them or can't care for them. Good shelters will spay or neuter and provide basic health care for the dogs in their care.

Shelters vary a great deal in their facilities, staff, and the time and attention they can put into each individual animal. Many Corgis will appear to be depressed or hyper, when they end up in a shelter. You can better evaluate the dog by asking to take her outside or to a quiet room for thirty minutes or so.

Adult Dogs from Breeders

Breeders will sometimes have an older puppy or an adult dog they want to rehome. Perhaps the Corgi is not going to be the top show dog they had hoped for. Now they want to put that dog in a loving home where she will be the star no matter what and get plenty of special attention. Family problems can also lead to a need to place well-trained, wonderful Corgis.

Part II

Caring for Your Corgi

Chapter 5

Bringing Home Your Pembroke Welsh Corgi

Bringing home a new family member is both very exciting and a bit stressful. Much of the information here is geared toward puppies, but it will also be true for a new adult dog.

The first few weeks in his new home are a critical period in your Corgi's life. To ensure that the transition goes smoothly and that both puppy and new family start off on the right foot, a little preplanning is advisable. Preparing in advance will make the transition to a new home as smooth as possible for everyone.

Before you bring your Corgi home, a few decisions need to be made. The whole family should agree on these decisions so the pup gets consistent care and training. Little puppies are still babies and need clear and consistent guidelines to help them adjust to life with their new family.

Where is he going to sleep? Where will he stay when you go out and he has to stay behind? Where will he go to the bathroom? Will he be allowed on the sofa? Who is going to feed him, when, and where? And most important, is he coming into your life when you have the extra time to enjoy his puppyhood?

Plan in advance, not on the spur of the moment. If you look at a housetraining schedule, puppy training classes, plus the time and effort a puppy needs and realize you truly can't add a new family member at this time, don't be afraid to say so. Better to decide that now than to end up dropping your Corgi at a shelter or a rescue group in six months.

> **TIP**
>
> Avoid adding a new puppy around a big holiday. Things are too exciting.

The Crate—a Room of His Own

The box on page 50 is a shopping list of things you'll need to have on hand before your new dog comes home. One of the most important items on that list is a crate.

Wild canines, especially puppies, spend a great deal of time in a cozy, secure den. You can provide a "civilized" version of this by giving your dog a crate to sleep in. A crate can also give you some control over your dog's whereabouts and will help with housetraining.

Corgis love crates. If your dog is introduced to his crate in a positive way, he will invariably use it as his own room, to be alone with a treasured toy or for a short snooze. Just supply a soft, washable blanket or towel and leave the door open. The crate can be placed in your dog's corner of the kitchen or wherever you have set up a special spot for him. Since Corgis are relatively small, their crates aren't large either. The crate can easily be moved from room to room so your puppy can be near you even when you can't watch him every second.

When your dog is going in the crate on his own, briefly shut the door. Your dog may fuss a bit at first when the crate door is shut. Each

Used properly, a crate will become your dog's safe haven.

time you put him in, supply a treat and a favorite toy. Tell him he is a good boy and disregard his clamor to escape. He will soon settle down. If you let him out immediately when he cries, he will have trained you to let him out on his command.

Crate Types

Crates can be made of heavy wire or plastic. Wire is cooler in warm weather. Plastic is required by airlines and is snug and lighter to carry. There are also canvas and cloth crates, but these should not be used for puppies because they can easily chew through them. They can be ideal for a well-trained adult, however.

Puppy Essentials

You'll need to go shopping *before* you bring your puppy home. There are many, many adorable and tempting items at pet supply stores, but these are the basics.

- **Food and water dishes.** Look for bowls that are wide and low or weighted in the bottom so they will be harder to tip over. Stainless steel bowls are a good choice because they are easy to clean (plastic never gets completely clean) and almost impossible to break. Avoid bowls that place the food and water side by side in one unit—it's too easy for your dog to get his water dirty that way.
- **Leash.** A six-foot leather leash will be easy on your hands and very strong.
- **Collar.** Start with a nylon buckle collar. For a perfect fit, you should be able to insert two fingers between the collar and your pup's neck. Your dog will need larger collars as he grows up.
- **Crate.** Choose a sturdy crate that is easy to clean and large enough for your puppy to stand up, turn around, and lie down in.
- **Nail cutters.** Get a good, sharp pair that are the appropriate size for the nails you will be cutting. Your dog's breeder or veterinarian can give you some guidance here.
- **Grooming tools.** Different kinds of dogs need different kinds of grooming tools. See chapter 7 for advice on what to buy.
- **Chew toys.** Dogs *must* chew, especially puppies. Make sure you get things that won't break or crumble off in little bits, which the dog can choke on. Very hard plastic bones are a good choice. Dogs love rawhide bones, too, but pieces of the rawhide can get caught in your dog's throat, so they should only be allowed when you are there to supervise.
- **Toys.** Watch for sharp edges and unsafe items such as plastic eyes that can be swallowed. Many toys come with squeakers, which dogs can also tear out and swallow. All dogs will eventually destroy their toys; as each toy is torn apart, replace it with a new one.

It is important to get the right size for an adult. The dog should be able to stand up and turn around in the crate. The dimensions should be approximately 27 inches long by 22 inches high by 17 inches wide. A big male might appreciate a little more room, but the crate loses its appeal as a den if it is too big.

Canine Bedding

Don't ask your dog to lie on the bare floor of the crate. It needs some bedding. There are many comfy dog beds on the market. Don't buy that expensive designer couch just yet, though. All puppies chew, so initially, be prepared to find any pillows or bedding shredded.

Imitation sheepskin as bedding is fairly sturdy, washable, and has dog appeal. Your dog's breeder may send a towel with the smell of her littermates and first home from their house to help your pup through the first couple of nights.

Responsible Crate Use

Crates are wonderful for all involved, but their use must not be abused. Be sure the dog gets a chance to exercise and eliminate before being confined. No dog, puppies in particular, should be locked in a crate for long periods during the day.

With young puppies, you can move the crate from room to room with you so the dog is not left alone. A good basic rule is that your puppy should not be in the crate without a break for more than an hour per month of age. So a 3-month-old Corgi pup should not be left in a crate for more than three hours. Ideally, no dog is in a crate for more than six hours at a time—and not that long every day.

In warm weather, your dog may need a bowl of water in his crate. You can find models that clip to the inside of the door. For dogs who tend to spill water, putting a few ice cubes in the bowl might be the best choice.

Choosing Toys and Chewies

All puppies go through a teething stage during which they act like fur-trimmed mouths. Have an ample supply of chew toys on hand to satisfy the puppy's natural urge to chew. Correct your puppy right away if he is chewing on something that belongs to you, then provide him with an acceptable chew item.

Chew Toys

Homemade playthings are free. A knotted rope, an empty paper towel roll, a cardboard egg carton, or a knotted sock will fascinate a puppy. Rawhide items are popular, but be careful that the softened, slimy pieces are not swallowed whole—they can choke a puppy.

It is best to always supervise your Corgi when he has a chew item that he might eat or destroy. Cow hooves, pig ears, and pork snouts can all cause health problems, and it is best to avoid them.

Choose sturdy chew toys that your dog can't shred and swallow.

Another option is hard nylon toys, which come in a variety of shapes and flavors. The hard rubber toys are also sturdy, safe chew toys. Commercial toys made of lengths of knotted rope are attractive to some pups. Make sure the dog is not shredding the rope and swallowing any of the string.

Corgis enjoy gnawing on a bone, but the wrong kind can splinter and injure the dog's mouth or digestive tract. Beware of hardened bones that are precooked and dried. These are very hard and brittle and may damage your Corgi's teeth. From the butcher you may occasionally get a fresh bone. The only acceptable fresh bone is cut from the shank of a beef leg bone, at least one and half inches long with no knuckle. Avoid other bones.

Other Toys

The array of available fuzzy toys and colorful latex or vinyl squeakies is mind-boggling. Mooing cows, soft sculpture hamburgers, prickly hedgehogs, politicans—you name it. These toys are as much for you as they are for your pup. Avoid toys with small parts (such as embedded eyes) that can be plucked out and swallowed. Be extremely careful with the squeakers. Corgis are adept at extracting them in a flash. If a vinyl or latex toy is being demolished, get rid of it. If toy pieces are swallowed, you should consult your veterinarian.

Do not offer your dog personal items such as an old shoe. He won't know a castoff from your expensive party shoes. Needless to say, anything left lying about on the floor is fair game to the puppy, so pick up any personal items.

To Tug or Not to Tug

Some behaviorists and trainers believe tug toys promote aggression and possessiveness and advise against playing tug-of-war games with a dog. However, recent studies show that tug games, done correctly, can be an excellent way to focus your puppy on you.

If you tug with your pup, you must be sure to reinforce an "out" (a command that means "let go when I say so") so that the pup drops the item when asked. Swap a small treat for the tug toy as a reward. If your Corgi tends to growl when tugging or won't stop when told, you should probably avoid tug games. *Never* lift your Corgi up by the tug toy! If you have doubts about whether to play tug with your dog, ask for guidance from an experienced dog trainer.

Outdoor Safety

It is not a good idea to turn your Corgi loose outside by himself. He could get hit by a car or attacked by another animal or stolen. Many communities now have leash laws. For peace of mind, a fenced yard is best.

Outdoors, your dog is safest in a fenced yard.

Puppy-Proofing Your Home

You can prevent much of the destruction puppies can cause and keep your new dog safe by looking at your home and yard from a dog's point of view. Get down on all fours and look around. Do you see loose electrical wires, cords dangling from the blinds, or chewable shoes on the floor? Your pup will see them too!

In the kitchen:
- Put all knives and other utensils away in drawers.
- Get a trash can with a tight-fitting lid.
- Put all household cleaners in cupboards that close securely; consider using childproof latches on the cabinet doors.

In the bathroom:
- Keep all household cleaners, medicines, vitamins, shampoos, bath products, perfumes, makeup, nail polish remover, and other personal products in cupboards that close securely; consider using childproof latches on the cabinet doors.
- Get a trash can with a tight-fitting lid.
- Don't use toilet bowl cleaners that release chemicals into the bowl every time you flush.
- Keep the toilet bowl lid down.
- Throw away potpourri and any solid air fresheners.

In the bedroom:
- Securely put away all potentially dangerous items, including medicines and medicine containers, vitamins and supplements, perfumes, and makeup.
- Put all your jewelry, barrettes, and hairpins in secure boxes.
- Pick up all socks, shoes, and other chewables.

In the rest of the house:

- Tape up or cover electrical cords; consider childproof covers for unused outlets.
- Knot or tie up any dangling cords from curtains, blinds, and the telephone.
- Securely put away all potentially dangerous items, including medicines and medicine containers, vitamins and supplements, cigarettes, cigars, pipes and pipe tobacco, pens, pencils, felt-tip markers, craft and sewing supplies, and laundry products.
- Put all houseplants out of reach.
- Move breakable items off low tables and shelves.
- Pick up all chewable items, including television and electronics remote controls, cell phones, MP3 players, shoes, socks, slippers and sandals, food, dishes, cups and utensils, toys, books and magazines, and anything else that can be chewed on.

In the garage:

- Store all gardening supplies and pool chemicals out of reach of the dog.
- Store all antifreeze, oil, and other car fluids securely, and clean up any spills by hosing them down for at least ten minutes.
- Put all dangerous substances on high shelves or in cupboards that close securely; consider using childproof latches on the cabinet doors.
- Pick up and put away all tools.
- Sweep the floor for nails and other small, sharp items.

In the yard:

- Put the gardening tools away after each use.
- Make sure the kids put away their toys when they're finished playing.
- Keep the pool covered or otherwise restrict your pup's access to it when you're not there to supervise.
- Secure the cords on backyard lights and other appliances.
- Inspect your fence thoroughly. If there are any gaps or holes in the fence, fix them.
- Make sure you have no toxic plants in the garden.

A Safe Yard

Fortunately, Corgis have short legs. Wire fencing that is only three feet high is enough to contain them. With a little ingenuity and at minor expense, an adequate pen can be arranged in just about any yard. The perfect setup is a fenced area large enough for the Corgi to be able to get up to running speed. Access should be via a convenient door, so the dog can remain close to the house while resting outdoors.

Remember that Corgis are excellent diggers, so check your fence line frequently for any attempts to tunnel out. Also check your fenced area for poisonous plants. Even with a safe yard, though, a Corgi should not be left alone outside during the day. If you are not home, he should be safely confined inside.

> **TIP**
>
> Another useful item to have is a pooper-scooper. Many communities have pick-up laws with serious fines. A small shovel and a paint stick certainly do the trick, but mini-shovels and rakes with long handles make this daily chore easier. An easy alternative is to carry a small plastic bag to scoop your dog's poop. Slip the bag over your hand, pick up, then turn the bag inside out over your hand and tie it shut.

Walking the Dog

Not everyone has a backyard or is able to provide the security of fencing. For these families, walking the dog is a way of life. Corgis thrive with the guaranteed bonding time that leash walking brings. If you use a retractable leash, your dog's walk will be a little more adventurous for her. Nonetheless, a good run in a safe place is always appreciated.

You may want to check out local dog parks and doggie day care centers. See if they have a separate small dog area so your young Corgi won't be overwhelmed by bigger dogs. Also be sure to ask about health concerns, such as vaccination requirements and fecal checks. Your Corgi should not go to any of those places until his puppy vaccination series is complete.

Meeting Other Pets

A little time and effort goes a long way when it comes to introducing your Corgi puppy to other pets in your household. If you have an older dog, you need to be very considerate of that dog. The older dog should have a quiet place to relax away from a badgering pup. He should get priority when it comes to who goes out the door first, who lies on the best bed, and so on. A young puppy will need a great deal of time simply due to his age, but make sure the older dog gets plenty of special attention so he won't resent the newcomer. With any luck, they will become best buddies.

A cat who has grown up with dogs can usually handle a puppy quite well. But if your pup has not been around cats or your cat has not been around dogs, you need to take precautions. Make sure the litter box is safely kept out of your puppy's reach. Also, your cat needs her normal quiet places to escape and rest. Creative use of baby gates works well. Pocket pets or house rabbits may need to be guarded from a wild and inquisitive pup as well.

Introductions are best made in neutral territory. Certainly your cat

Introduce a new dog to a resident dog in neutral territory.

doesn't have to go to the park to meet the puppy, but it might be a good place for your older dog and the pup to meet. Have help to restrain any of the animals, if need be. Be careful—you don't want anyone getting scratched or bitten.

Having the pup in a crate that other dogs or a cat can then approach and sniff can also work well.

Establish a Routine

Every dog thrives on routine: when to get up, when to go out, when to eat and where, and when it's bedtime. Doing the same thing at approximately the same time every day provides a comfortable continuity and reduces stress.

Your Corgi's schedule might include trips outside first thing in the morning, last thing at night, after each meal, after each nap during the day, and whatever time in between that he looks as if he needs to relieve himself.

Your Corgi will benefit from having a regular schedule. That should include plenty of naps for puppies.

Your dog should be fed at regular times each day and in the same place. Puppies between 3 and 6 months of age should be fed three times a day and given a biscuit at bedtime. If the pup is only 8 weeks old, four meals a day may be appropriate. Once he reaches 6 months, twice a day is fine. Most Corgis prefer two meals a day throughout their lives, and there are some health and behavior benefits.

When planning a schedule for your Corgi, be sure to allow plenty of time for him to sleep. Puppies play hard and then drop. Do not disturb! A puppy who is constantly revved up in play and never allowed to simmer down and rest becomes a neurotic, hyper adult. Make sure your kids understand and follow this rule!

Set the Rules from the Start

Corgis, being the clever little creatures they are, need to learn straight off that no back talk is allowed. A Corgi with the upper paw can become a tyrant. Growling is not cute at any age. Do not let the puppy get away with anything that you would not like a grown dog to do.

Set rules for polite interaction right from the start.

If your Corgi resists being handled or snarls and nips, sternly say "No!" and hold him gently but firmly. Act calm as he carries on, and put him down only when he has quieted. Do this when he is young, and he will be easy to handle under difficult circumstances when he grows up.

Never allow your Corgi to get his way through bad behavior. As always, you make the decisions. Make sure the entire family knows and abides by your rules. For example, if the family decides no dog on the sofa, that rule should hold no matter who is home.

Do not let a new puppy have the run of the house when he first comes home. Bad habits are quickly acquired and hard to break. It is best to start small and then gradually expand your pup's horizons as training and bladder control progress. In the early stages, he should be brought into the living room only for brief periods under the watchful eye of an adult or confined to his crate. (Chapter 10 outlines a plan for housetraining.)

Chapter 6

Feeding Your Pembroke Welsh Corgi

The old adage "You are what you eat" applies to Pembroke Welsh Corgis as well as humans. And if there is one thing virtually all Corgis agree on, it is that food is wonderful! Since Corgis tend to be easy keepers and will eat almost anything, it is your job to be sure your Corgi has an excellent diet and in just the right amount. One of the most important things to remember about feeding your Corgi is that each Corgi should be fed as an individual.

The Essentials

There are some dietary ingredients that are essential for a healthy Corgi. These things must be included in the diet and in a digestible form.

- **Protein.** Your Corgi needs good quality protein in her diet. That means she needs a certain amount of protein and it must also contain the necessary amino acids that are building blocks for so many tissues and enzymes in her body. Dogs have ten essential amino acids that must be included in their diet. The amount of protein dogs need may vary with life stage, activity levels, and health status. Proteins are found in meats, fish, eggs, dairy products, and legumes, especially beans.
- **Carbohydrates.** Carbohydrates are a source of energy for most dogs and may provide fiber to help with digestion. Carbohydrates come from plant sources such as grains.

Water is a vital part of your dog's diet. Make sure she always has fresh, clean water available.

- **Fats.** Fats are important in your Corgi's diet for energy, skin, and coat health, and for metabolizing certain vitamins. Most dogs love fats, but too much fat in the diet is not healthy. Luckily, dogs do not develop the same cholesterol problems that we humans do, but too much fat can cause diarrhea.
- **Minerals.** Minerals are important for enzyme functions, work with many vitamins, build bones, and keep muscles working properly, among other duties. They are very important for many metabolic functions. While minerals may only need to be present in the diet in small amounts, they must be correctly balanced. For example, your Corgi needs just the right ratio of calcium and phosphorus to have healthy bone growth.
- **Vitamins.** Vitamins are another small but important part of your Corgi's diet. Many vitamins work with nutrients or minerals to keep the body healthy. Too much of most vitamins is as bad as too little, so these must be balanced as well.
- **Water.** Water seems like such a simple, almost silly thing to list, but water is even more important than food. Your Corgi needs plenty of fresh, clean water available all the time. Most dogs prefer their water cold, as well. Your Corgi would die of dehydration long before she would starve to death, so make sure she always has water!

Choosing a Dog Food

Dog foods come in different forms. The two most common forms are canned and dry. Most Corgis find canned foods to be very tasty. Canned foods will contain more moisture and can be stored longer without problems. Some canned foods are primarily meat and are not balanced by themselves. They need to be combined with another food.

Dry foods are baked or cooked. These foods tend to be less expensive and may contain more grains. Semimoist foods tend to have large amounts of sugar and preservatives and are not generally recommended.

In general, the more expensive foods use higher quality ingredients and have consistent recipes that are followed. While the cost may seem higher at first, due to the top quality most Corgis thrive on a smaller amount of these foods, so in the long run these foods are well worth it.

Special Diets

Some dogs have health problems that respond at least in part to dietary management. These dogs may need a special prescription diet as part of their medical care. This could be a diet with top-quality but restricted amounts of protein or added fiber for digestion control. Nonprescription special diets include diets aimed at helping your overweight dog lose some weight. Most of these diets are not appropriate for puppies.

Check with your veterinarian if you feel your Corgi might benefit from a special diet or a change in diet. For some health problems, a home-cooked diet following a recipe from a veterinary nutritionist might be just the thing.

Supplements and Additives

In general, there is no need to add vitamin and mineral supplements to a premium, top-quality commercially prepared dog food. The nutritional balance of the product will be disturbed if nutrients are added. It takes considerable knowledge to properly supplement your dog's diet with vitamins and minerals. When not administered in precise ratios and amounts, they can be detrimental instead of helpful.

Still, a balanced vitamin-mineral complex or other supplement may be helpful for some Corgis. The key word is "balanced." Your veterinarian can suggest specific brands that will be best for your Corgi. For example, some dogs will have an improvement in coat quality by adding the right types of fatty acids to their diet.

Reading Dog Food Labels

Dog food labels are not always easy to read, but if you know what to look for they can tell you a lot about what your dog is eating.

- The label should have a statement saying the dog food meets or exceeds the Association of American Feed Control Officials (AAFCO) nutritional guidelines. If the dog food doesn't meet AAFCO guidelines, it can't be considered complete and balanced, and can cause nutritional deficiencies.
- The guaranteed analysis lists the minimum percentages of crude protein and crude fat and the maximum percentages of crude fiber and water. AAFCO requires a minimum of 18 percent crude protein for adult dogs and 22 percent crude protein for puppies on a dry matter basis (that means with the water removed; canned foods will have less protein because they have more water). Dog food must also have a minimum of 5 percent crude fat for adults and 8 percent crude fat for puppies.
- The ingredients list the most common item in the food first, and so on until you get to the least common item, which is listed last.
- Look for a dog food that lists an animal protein source first, such as chicken or poultry meal, beef or beef byproducts, and that has other protein sources listed among the top five ingredients. That's because a food that lists chicken, wheat, wheat gluten, corn, and wheat fiber as the first five ingredients has more chicken than wheat, but may not have more chicken than all the grain products put together.
- Other ingredients may include a carbohydrate source, fat, vitamins and minerals, preservatives, fiber, and sometimes other additives purported to be healthy.
- Some brands may add artificial colors, sugar, and fillers—all of which should be avoided.

Fresh Foods and Homemade Diets

Fresh food can be added to a basic commercial diet in small amounts. Corgis enjoy small pieces of raw vegetables, berries, apples, bananas, and other noncitrus fruits. You can also add small amounts of cooked chicken, fish, or

A dog eating a high-quality, well-formulated diet will not need extra supplements and additives.

hamburger. Egg yolks are easily digestible and a super source of protein, but eggs should be cooked before serving. Cottage cheese is also a good nutritional source. Growing puppies, pregnant and nursing bitches, convalescent dogs, and those stressed with a heavy show schedule might benefit from these extra additives for optimum condition.

To maintain the desired proper balanced diet, no more than 15 percent of any meal should be made up of these special items.

You can also cook complete meals for your Corgi or feed a raw diet. Some families will purchase freeze-dried or frozen meats or meals and mix them up themselves to make a balanced diet. Raw diets are now also available commercially in prepared formulas. If you choose to cook at home or to feed a raw diet, you need to consult a veterinary nutritionist to be sure you have balanced meals. You must also use extreme care in your food preparations to avoid food poisoning.

Feeding During Different Stages

A dog requires different nutrients, different amounts of fat and protein, and different-size meals during the various stages of her life. Here are some tips on how to feed your dog appropriately.

Pet Food vs. People Food

Many of the foods we eat are excellent sources of nutrients—after all, we do just fine on them. But dogs, like us, need the right combination of meat and other ingredients for a complete and balanced diet, and a bowl of meat doesn't provide that. In the wild, dogs eat the fur, skin, bones, and guts of their prey, and even the contents of the stomach.

This doesn't mean your dog can't eat what you eat. A little meat, dairy, bread, some fruits, or vegetables as a treat are great. Just remember, we're talking about the same food you eat, not the gristly, greasy leftovers you would normally toss in the trash. Stay away from sugar, too, and remember that chocolate and alcohol are toxic to dogs.

If you want to share your food with your dog, be sure the total amount you give her each day doesn't make up more than 15 percent of her diet, and that the rest of what you feed her is a top-quality complete and balanced dog food. (More people food could upset the balance of nutrients in the commercial food.)

Can your dog eat an entirely homemade diet? Certainly, if you are willing to work at it. Any homemade diet will have to be carefully balanced, with all the right nutrients in just the right amounts. It requires a lot of research to make a proper homemade diet, but it can be done. It's best to work with a veterinary nutritionist.

Feeding a Puppy

When you picked up your pup from the breeder, you probably were given an information sheet telling what, how much, and when she was used to eating. Ideally, you were sent home with a few days' supply of your puppy's food. Follow the breeder's instructions closely to minimize the digestive stress to your puppy. If you would like to change the food, do so very gradually over several

Growing puppies need more protein, calories, and fat in their diet than adult dogs need.

days so that her stomach will not be upset. Mix the two foods over time, gradually decreasing the old and increasing the new.

The amount you feed your Corgi puppy will change as she grows. Monitor her growth and make sure she is not overweight, as this will put extra stress on her developing joints. Most puppies do best with three meals daily—morning, noon, and night. At about 5 or 6 months of age, the noon meal can be discontinued.

Feeding an Adult

After your dog's first birthday, switch from the puppy formula to an adult maintenance food. Adult dogs do best on two meals a day. Many Corgis have great internal clocks and will remind you of their meal times. If you need to change the diet, do so gradually over a few weeks. Check with your veterinarian before adding any supplements. And remember, each Corgi needs to be fed as an individual.

How Much Food?

Individual dogs vary in how much they should eat to maintain a desired body weight—not too fat but not too thin. Determine how much food keeps your adult dog looking and feeling her best. Remember that the amounts on dog food labels are just guidelines and that each dog needs to be fed as an individual.

Once you have decided on the total daily amount of food, divide it equally among the number of meals your dog gets each day. If you're worried about overfeeding, make sure you measure correctly and avoid between-meal snacking.

For each meal, leave your dog's food out only for the amount of time it takes her to eat it—about ten minutes. Free feeding (when food's available any time) and leisurely meals encourage picky eating and may lead to obesity problems.

Treats

Virtually all Corgis love treats, and this love of food provides you with an easy way to motivate your Corgi in training. The treats you use for training can be some of your dog's regular kibble or special training

> **TIP**
>
> If your Corgi has certain dietary restrictions, such as no wheat in her diet, you need to follow those guidelines in her treats as well.

treats. Remember that Corgis are not large dogs, so training treats should be small. You also need to count the treats as part of the food your Corgi eats every day. Otherwise she will get overweight.

The Chubby Corgi

Keeping your dog at her proper weight is not always easy. Corgis rapidly become obese, and this is bad for their general health. Your dog should have enough flesh to cover her bones. When looking down from above, your Corgi should have a "waist" right in front of her hip bones. You should also be able to feel her ribs easily without having to push through a thick layer of tissue.

Corgis are not picky eaters and tend to put on weight, so choose healthy snacks and treats for your dog. This dog is eating apple slices.

Many Corgis have "starving eyes." They look at you with their sweet expression and all you see is the darling dog who would love one more small treat. Sadly, those treats add up and then you have a round and unhealthy Corgi.

Time for a Diet!

Any Corgi over 32 pounds, no matter how large her bone structure, is fat. Accustom your eyes to the right look and be hard-hearted when she agitates for more tidbits. Generally speaking, females need to consume less than males to maintain the optimum weight.

Of course, the amount of exercise a dog gets and the quality of the ingredients in her dinner are factors involved in the perfect food equation. Watch your dog's body condition and adjust her diet accordingly. If things get out of control, talk to your veterinarian, who can prescribe a scientifically formulated diet to promote weight loss.

Many Corgis who agitate strongly for extra food do well with a tablespoon of plain canned pumpkin (no sugar and spice added) added to their food. The pumpkin is primarily fiber, so your Corgi feels full without a lot of extra calories.

When you're traveling with your dog, whether for fun or competition, bring along her usual food to avoid stomach upsets.

Also, research has shown that dogs can count. So if your Corgi generally gets two small biscuits before bed each night and you drop to one biscuit, she may hassle you endlessly. Take that one biscuit and break it in half; your Corgi is now happy and is still losing weight.

Foods to Avoid

Corgis are, for the most part, cheerful omnivores. That means they will eat almost anything. But there are a few items that, tempting as they may be, are *truly* bad for them. According to the ASPCA, the following foods and beverages are toxic to dogs:

> **TIP**
>
> Remember, table scraps can easily unbalance a healthy diet. If you want to deter begging, *never* slip a scrap to your dog under the dining room table. Begging is a vice that is easy to learn but hard to eliminate.

- Alcoholic beverages: Even a small amount can cause serious intoxication and be deadly.
- Chocolate and coffee (all forms): Chocolate and coffee contain caffeine and theobromine, a compound that is a cardiac stimulant and a diuretic, which causes vomiting, rapid breathing, seizures, and sometimes death.
- Fatty foods: Fatty and fried foods can cause liver damage. Turkey or chicken skin will invariably upset the stomach, as well.
- Onions and garlic: These contain the toxic ingredient thiosulphate, a substance that can break down red blood cells.
- Grapes and raisins: Grapes and raisins can cause vomiting, diarrhea, abdominal pain, and lethargy.
- Macadamia nuts: Macadamia nuts can cause weakness, muscle tremor and weakness, or paralysis in the hindquarters.
- Milk: Milk may cause diarrhea. As an alternative, canned or powdered milk is generally fine and useful for baby puppies who are being weaned. Most Corgis handle plain yogurt and cheese, as well.
- Spicy foods: These can cause digestive upsets.
- Uncooked yeast dough: Rising yeast dough can lead to digestive system upsets.
- Products sweetened with xylitol: Xylitol is an artificial sweetener used in diet products. It can cause a sudden drop in blood sugar, resulting in liver problems.

Chapter 7

Grooming Your Pembroke Welsh Corgi

The Welsh farmers of Pembrokeshire had no time to spend on the appearance of their all-purpose little helpers. An occasional bath when it was obviously necessary or maybe a quick swipe with a brush after returning from a muddy pasture was all those Corgis could expect. Fortunately, because their coats naturally repel dirt when it dries, they kept themselves fairly clean.

Corgi owners today are grateful for this legacy. Corgis, with their wash-and-wear coats, are easy to groom. Still, since Corgis are fairly low to the ground, you can expect them to pick up dirt and mud on a walk. Also, for a small dog, Corgis can really shed. That wonderful double coat, with coarse guard hairs over a thick undercoat, provides plenty of loose hair during shedding season. Many dogs shed in both spring and fall, but intact females will shed around their heat cycles. Corgis who live indoors may shed all year long.

Basic Combing and Brushing

Set aside some time for brushing at least once a week. Corgis do shed, and dead hair can accumulate in their coats and all over your house. A short weekly or twice weekly grooming session is much more fun for both you and your Corgi than a monthly marathon. Your Corgi's skin will be healthier with regular grooming, plus he will look great. Regular grooming provides a bonding time between person and dog, as well, which is usually enjoyed by both.

During the weekly grooming session, check his skin for sore spots, cuts, and parasites. It's also wise to give your dog a good once-over with a fine-toothed comb after each walk in the woods, to check for fleas and ticks.

When grooming becomes a weekly routine, it will be hassle-free. Your dog will know what to expect, and more important, he will have learned to be handled and held without fussing. For a puppy, daily two-minute sessions are best until he is comfortable with the grooming procedure and can handle staying still.

Where to Groom

With a short dog, you may be more comfortable having him elevated so you don't have to bend over. Many people groom their Corgis on a sturdy grooming table that has a nonslip top surface. You can buy a grooming table from pet supply catalogs, the Internet, or at dog shows. Or it can be a handyman's project.

You can also use an old folding table. Just make sure it's sturdy and not wobbly. And put a nonslip mat on top so your dog feels safe and secure.

Any dog on a table must be watched constantly to prevent a fall or ill-fated jump. *Never* leave your Corgi unattended on a grooming table!

It's just as satisfactory to sit with your dog on the floor for his grooming session. Set out a towel, position yourself on one end, and let him settle down between your outspread legs with his head toward your feet.

Have your grooming tools at hand, along with a wastebasket or a bag for the dead hair. You will need a steel comb with wide- and thin-spaced teeth, a fine-toothed flea comb, and a natural bristle brush. During the winter, using a spray bottle filled with plain water helps control static.

How to Groom

Start with the wide-spaced side of the comb. Work from the top of the neck down the back and over the sides, following the natural lie of the hair. Take fairly short, deep strokes and be careful that you don't scratch the dog's skin. Continue combing until the comb goes through the hair easily. It often takes a bit of a tug over the rump. Repeat with the fine-spaced side of the comb. Once you have combed over an area, repeat with the bristle brush. You may need to spray the coat periodically with plain water to reduce static. If the comb has trouble going through, you may need to use the brush first.

Grooming Tools

Steel comb with fine- and medium-spaced teeth

Fine-toothed flea comb

Natural bristle brush

Guillotine-style nail clipper and/or electric nail grinder

Trimming scissors

Cotton balls

Tooth-cleaning equipment

pH balanced shampoo

Towels

It's much easier to groom a short dog on a raised surface. If you don't want to buy a grooming table, put an old towel on a sturdy folding table.

Gently place your dog on his side. Use the wide-spaced teeth and start at the shoulder. If the comb has trouble getting through the coat, start with the bristle brush first. Always comb the hair in the direction in which it grows. When combing the sides, it's easiest to do small sections from the thinner belly hair up to the top. Again, repeat with the narrow teeth. Do not forget the legs, belly, and feathering (the longer, fluffier hair) at the rear legs. Turn your dog over and do the other side. Finally, comb the ruff. Fluff it up with the brush.

Another way to work through the coat, especially if the undercoat is very thick, is to start at the back. Hold a section of hair back with one hand and, little by little, comb the lowest layer straight out. This works particularly well for the feathering. Slowly work forward.

It can be very tempting to just brush or comb the dog's back. Don't give in to that temptation. Always make sure you brush and comb the sides and underneath as well as on top.

External Parasites

During your regular grooming sessions, be sure to use a flea comb to catch fleas and ticks. If the coat has not already been combed through, it is very hard to get a flea comb through it. So make this the last step in your grooming routine. If you trap a flea in the comb, kill it by squeezing it against your thumbnail or submerge it in a cup of water. Ticks should be removed as described in the box on page 77.

Fleas

The adult flea is a small, brown insect about an eighth of an inch long. It can easily be seen hurrying along through your dog's fur. Fleas can jump and run quickly. Even if you do not catch a glimpse of a flea, you can tell just by looking that they are living on your Corgi when you find tiny specks of black dirt on the skin. This is dried blood excreted by these bloodsucking insects. When a wet tissue is applied to these dots, they will turn red.

Many Corgis have only a mild reaction to fleas. Others are hypersensitive to flea saliva and suffer greatly from severe skin reactions and the resultant hot spots. Fleas are not only a nuisance; a severe infestation can result in anemia due to blood loss. Fleas can also transmit tapeworms.

Any outdoor space can harbor fleas and ticks. That includes your backyard.

Getting rid of fleas is a challenge. Effective flea control requires treating the environment as well as the dog. The dog can be washed and/or combed free of the critters, but he will not stay that way if fleas are hanging around the house, yard, and car. See the box on page 74 for more information on keeping fleas off your dog.

Ticks

The ticks that most commonly attach themselves to dogs are the brown dog tick and the deer tick. As an adult, the brown dog tick about the size of a flat match head. An engorged female looks like a gray raisin.

Making Your Environment Flea Free

If there are fleas on your dog, there are fleas in your home, yard, and car, even if you can't see them. Take these steps to combat them.

In your home:

- Wash whatever is washable (the dog bed, sheets, blankets, pillow covers, slipcovers, curtains, etc.).
- Vacuum everything else in your home—furniture, floors, rugs, everything. Pay special attention to the folds and crevices in upholstery, the cracks between floorboards, and the spaces between the floor and the baseboards. Flea larvae are sensitive to sunlight, so inside the house they prefer deep carpet, bedding, and cracks and crevices.
- When you're done, throw the vacuum cleaner bag away—in an outside garbage can.
- Use a nontoxic flea-killing powder to treat your carpets (but remember, it does not control fleas elsewhere in the house). The powder stays deep in the carpet and kills fleas (using a form of boric acid) for up to a year.
- If you have a particularly serious flea problem, consider using a fogger or long-lasting spray to kill any adult and larval fleas, or having a professional exterminator treat your home.

Deer ticks are extremely small, dark brown walking dots. They remain quite small even when engorged. In their larval stage, they are minute. (Look for them on the dog's eyelids.) Ticks are dangerous not only because their bites can leave sores but because of the diseases they may be carrying. Rocky Mountain spotted fever, ehrlichiosis, and Lyme disease, among others, are transmitted by ticks. It is important to keep a close watch for ticks and remove them as soon as possible, preferably before they have had time to embed themselves in your dog.

Mites

There are assorted mites that can cause serious skin problems, including sarcoptic and demodectic mange. If your dog has scaly, bare patches of skin that become red and itchy, whisk him to the veterinarian, who can make a diagnosis through a skin scraping. Sarcoptic mange is treatable, but demodectic mange can be very difficult to control.

In your car:

- Take out the floor mats and hose them down with a strong stream of water, then hang them up to dry in the sun.
- Wash any towels, blankets, or other bedding you regularly keep in the car.
- Thoroughly vacuum the entire interior of your car, paying special attention to the seams between the bottom and back of the seats.
- When you're done, throw the vacuum cleaner bag away—in an outside garbage can.

In your yard:

- Flea larvae prefer shaded areas that have plenty of organic material and moisture, so rake the yard thoroughly and bag all the debris in tightly sealed bags.
- Spray your yard with an insecticide that has residual activity for at least thirty days. Insecticides that use a form of boric acid are nontoxic. Some products contain an insect growth regulator (such as fenoxycarb) and need to be applied only once or twice a year.
- For an especially difficult flea problem, consider having an exterminator treat your yard.
- Keep your yard free of piles of leaves, weeds, and other organic debris. Be especially careful in shady, moist areas, such as under bushes.

Shedding

Unspayed bitches will go through an epic shed that is known as *blowing coat.* This thorough molt is triggered by hormone changes associated with their seasons or maternal duties. The hair comes out in handfuls. A mom who has just given birth is so naked there is nothing to do but laugh. The boys and spayed bitches also go "out of coat," but not as often as intact females. Their shedding season tends to follow the seasons, with some heavy shedding in spring and fall.

Whenever you notice that the coat looks dry and little tufts of loose undercoat stick out on the shoulders or haunches, beware—it's going to be a hairy few weeks. You can actually pluck the hair clumps out of the coat. Now is the time to thoroughly comb and brush your dog every day or two. Pull out any loose

New Products in the Fight Against Fleas

At one time, battling fleas meant exposing your dog and your-self to toxic dips, sprays, powders, and collars. But today there are flea preventives that work very well and are safe for your dog, you, and the environment. The two most common types are insect growth regulators (IGRs), which stop the immature flea from developing or maturing, and adult flea killers. To deal with an active infestation, experts usually recommend a product that has both.

These next-generation flea fighters generally come in one of two forms:

- **Topical treatments or spot-ons.** These products are applied to the skin, usually between the shoulder blades. The product is absorbed through the skin into the dog's system.
- **Systemic products.** This is a pill your dog swallows that transmits a chemical throughout the dog's bloodstream. When a flea bites the dog, it picks up this chemical, which then prevents the flea's eggs from developing.

Talk to your veterinarian about which product is best for your dog. Make sure you read all the labels and apply the products exactly as recommended, and that you check to make sure they are safe for puppies.

clumps as they appear. When the old coat is almost gone, a warm bath hastens the rest of the molt.

The guard hairs along the spine are the last to go. While a shedding Corgi may not look his best, once the older, dull hairs are gone, he will be shiny and handsome.

How to Get Rid of a Tick

Although many of the new generation of flea fighters are partially effective in killing ticks once they are on your dog, they are not 100 percent effective and will not keep ticks from biting your dog in the first place. During tick season (which, depending on where you live, can be spring, summer, and/or fall), examine your dog every day for ticks. Pay particular attention to your dog's neck, behind the ears, the armpits, and the groin.

When you find a tick, use a pair of tweezers to grasp the tick as close as possible to the dog's skin and pull it out using firm, steady pressure. Check to make sure you get the whole tick (mouth parts left in your dog's skin can cause an infection), then wash the wound and dab it with a little antibiotic ointment. Watch for signs of inflammation.

Ticks carry very serious diseases that are transmittable to humans, so dispose of the tick safely. *Never* crush it between your fingers. Don't flush it down the toilet either, because the tick will survive the trip and infect another animal. Instead, use the tweezers to place the tick in a tight-sealing jar or plastic dish with a little alcohol, put on the lid, and dispose of the container in an outdoor garbage can. Wash the tweezers thoroughly with hot water and alcohol.

Managing a Fluffy

A Corgi with a fluffy coat of lengthy, silky hair requires more grooming than a standard-coated one. This type of hair does not shed dirt readily. It collects grass, twigs, and burrs, and may mat easily. A brush is useful to start the grooming process. Work from the back forward, and bottom to top, holding the hair up and smoothing one layer at a time.

Watch out for mats, particularly behind the ears and under the forearms. Mats pull the skin and hurt when brushed, or when the dog moves. It may be

Corgis tend to shed more heavily in the spring and fall, and their coats will need extra attention.

The fluffies will need more grooming—and probably more frequent baths, as well.

necessary to cut them out. If your Corgi becomes badly matted, he may need to be shaved. Daily sessions of combing and brushing for even a minute or two can prevent that.

Combing a neglected fluffy can be quite a project and may take more than one session. If it becomes too much for you, take the dog to a groomer. A little judicious scissoring here and there may help.

Other Weekly Chores

Grooming your dog isn't just a way to keep him looking pretty. It's also a time when you can make sure he is healthy. Your dog's weekly grooming session is a perfect time to check his eyes, ears, and teeth. Your Corgi has two eyes and two ears, so if you aren't sure whether something is normal, check the other side.

Keeping the Eyes Clean

Use a cotton ball to wipe away any excess tearing below the eye. If it is extensive or appears puslike, contact your veterinarian, who can prescribe medication and prevent more serious eye problems from developing. This also applies to a red or inflamed eye. If your Corgi is squinting, seek help at once. Your Corgi should not have constant drainage from the eyes, even if the fluid is clear and watery.

Many Corgis get dust and pollen in their eyes when running through dirt or grass, since they are low to the ground. It can be helpful to flush your Corgi's eyes with artificial tears after a romp outdoors in tall grass or dusty conditions.

Checking the Ears

Corgis do not seem to have the ear problems that plague many other breeds. At grooming time, wipe out any dirt or wax from the outer part of the ear with a special ear wipe or a damp, not wet, cloth. Never put a cotton swab down the ear canal. If there is a crusty brown discharge or the ear has an unpleasant odor, see your veterinarian.

Dental Check

Do a weekly check of your dog's mouth. Bad breath, tooth decay, loss of teeth, and periodontitis are widespread in the canine community. Attention to the teeth at grooming time will go a long way to prevent these problems.

When you groom your dog, gently wipe his ears and eyes with a clean, damp cloth.

Right from the start, get your dog accustomed to having his teeth cleaned. You do not need to open your Corgi's mouth very wide. You can simply reach in under the lips to get to the teeth and gums. Take a piece of gauze or terrycloth with a bit of dog toothpaste on it and wipe the plaque off his teeth. Doggy toothbrushes and toothpaste are available at pet supply stores. Do not use toothpaste designed for humans. The pet versions are made to be safely swallowed and come in a variety of flavors. Most Corgis seem to like the chicken flavor.

If your Corgi resists having his mouth examined, or if you feel uncomfortable cleaning his teeth, ask your veterinarian or a veterinary technician to show you how to do this. Eventually, most dogs will need a professional cleaning by a veterinarian.

Nail Detail

If your dog's paws are clicking across the floor, it is time to trim the nails. Neglecting the nails will cause the feet to splay, affect his gait, and eventually cause lameness if they grow so long that they curl back into his pads. Ideally, the nails should clear the floor when the dog is standing. To keep them this way usually means trimming at least every two weeks.

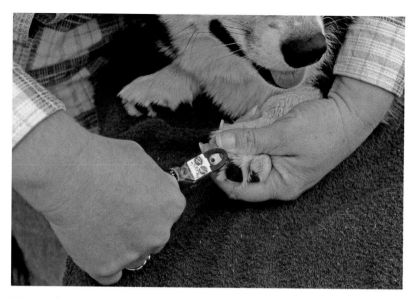

Use the guillotine-type nail clippers to trim just the tips of the nails.

It is not hard to learn how to safely trim your dog's nails. A pink quick runs down the center of each nail. If you cut this part, it can bleed and hurt. Fortunately, most Corgis have white paws with white nails, so the quick is visible in good light and can be avoided.

Most people prefer a guillotine-type nail trimmer. The blade slides up when you close the handle. Be sure you work in good light. Until you get the hang of it, snip off only the hooks at the end of the nail. Be very careful. If you draw blood, use styptic powder, a pinch of cornstarch, or even a bar of soap to stop the bleeding.

You probably will have to put your arm around the dog to steady him, but apply only as much pressure as is needed to keep him still. Corgis are more frightened by being held tightly than by the clipping process. Reassure your dog that he is a good boy. Do only a little at a time if he is unhappy, but do not let him decide when you are going to stop. Give him a good hug when you are finished.

A good way to trim nails is to sit on the floor with your dog on his back, steadied between your knees. Work from the underside of the nail and start the blade near the tip. Again, hold him only as tightly as necessary, pat him calmly, and do not tense up yourself. If there is a struggle, rest until he quiets down and then continue. Do not accept bad behavior or give up when he dictates. When you are done, hold him in your arms and pat him until he relaxes and is soaking up the affection. With this approach, your dog will soon be quite comfortable with nail trimming and might even volunteer.

Try the Grinder

Many dog owners prefer to grind the nails with a high-speed, handheld electric tool. These can be purchased at a hardware store or through a dog supply catalog or the Internet. They are light, small, and can be cordless. Look for at least 25,000 rpm (revolutions per minute) as the top speed.

The advantage of using a grinder is that you have tremendous control and can shorten the nail all the way to the quick without drawing any blood. Dogs may prefer the grinder over other trimming devices (once they become accustomed to the sound).

Stroke the nail lightly with the grinder and shift from nail to nail after just a few passes to avoid heat buildup from the friction. If you have not trimmed the nails for a few weeks, a combination of clipping the tips and grinding the rest will save time. You must be very careful when using the grinder not to go too short. You will not have any bleeding to indicate when you get near the quick.

Trim the Feet

While you're trimming nails, every so often trim the hair on your dog's feet. Use your scissors to remove the growth under the pads and neaten up the edges along the sides, but do not cut the hair too high on the paw. Older or infirm dogs benefit from the improved traction of trimmed feet, especially on slippery floors. Neat feet look nicer and pick up less dirt and mud. Also, if you trim nails with a grinder, be sure the hair is trimmed or it can get caught up in the grinder.

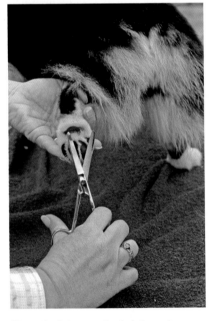

Use a pair of scissors to trim the hair growing between the pads.

Avoid the Fuss

Many Corgis are very bad about having their nails trimmed. This can be avoided by using some extra time and patience with your puppy. You can easily hold your puppy and simply trim one or two nails at a time, or just one foot. Then put the puppy down, reward him, and let him play. Do another foot or couple of nails the next day. This way he does not have to be still for a long period of time and he has good associations with the trimming.

Bath Time

It's not necessary to give your Corgi frequent baths. With adequate grooming, he will keep himself clean for quite a while. If his bedding is laundered and he is toweled off on rainy days, he won't acquire a doggy odor. However, a healthy sudsing will freshen the skin and make the coat sparkle. Choose a shampoo that is formulated for dogs. Do not shampoo your dog with products designed for humans, because they can dry the skin.

Washing removes the natural oils in the coat, so hair will not lie flat for a few days. Keep this in mind if you are planning to take your dog to a dog show. Give him his bath several days in advance.

Gather several absorbent towels, a washcloth, a comb, a dryer, and the shampoo. You have a choice of the bathtub, the kitchen sink, or a special tub to wash your little Corgi. A spray hose attachment is a decided advantage.

Washing Your Dog

The water should be lightly warm to the touch, almost tepid. Put him in the tub or sink. Some people advocate putting cotton balls in the ears to keep the water out.

Start by wetting your dog all over except for the head. Pour out some shampoo and lather up a ring around the neck. Work the shampoo into the back, down the sides, and on his chest and belly. Pick up each leg and wash it. Be sure to clean him down to the skin. A second soaping usually is not necessary.

With a cloth dampened with plain water, wipe out the insides of the ears. Wiping the face with a damp cloth is usually fine, as well. You don't want to get soap in his eyes, because it stings.

Rinse and Dry

When you've finished washing, thoroughly rinse your dog with lots of fresh water. It is critical to remove all the soap to prevent itchy skin. This may take quite a while.

Next, using at least two towels, dry him as best you can, then carry him to a spot where you can plug in the hair dryer. Do not use the dryer on high heat. It is best to get a blow dryer designed for dogs. Many Corgis will dry just fine with a few shakes and some warm towels. Puppies often are frightened by the dryer, but older dogs learn to enjoy the warmth.

Do not blow air into your Corgi's ears or on his face. Blow-dry the back first and then the belly. With the comb or a brush, separate the hair clumps. The areas over the hocks and behind the ears dry slowly, and a thick ruff is the last to dry. Do not forget to dry the legs and feet. With the combination of the comb or brush and the dryer, your dog will soon be gorgeous and squeaky clean.

Deskunking!

A bath is definitely needed if your Corgi has a close encounter with a skunk. This recipe works extremely well. Be sure to make it up fresh when needed, because it does not store well.

1 quart hydrogen peroxide (3-percent solution)
¼ cup baking soda
2 tablespoons dish soap (Dawn or Sunlight work particularly well)

Mix these ingredients and pour over your Corgi, rubbing into the coat. Leave on a minute or two, then rinse thoroughly.

Chapter 8

Keeping Your Pembroke Welsh Corgi Healthy

The buzzword in human health care is preventive medicine. This is also true for veterinary medicine. Some sensible preventive care can help keep your Corgi happy and healthy well into her teens. There are a few Corgi-specific health problems you need to be aware of. For information about senior dogs, see the online chapter at www.wiley.com/go/pembrokewelshcorgi.

Selecting a Veterinarian

Your first step in a lifetime of good health for your dog is choosing a veterinarian. Your veterinarian should be well-educated, knowledgeable, and up-to-date. Your veterinarian should enjoy dogs and be able and willing to explain your Corgi's care to you. Together, you are partners in your dog's health care.

Also look for a convenient location that you can reach easily in case of an emergency. Ask about emergency coverage for nights, weekends, and holidays. Most clinics will provide full care for your Corgi—including nutritional advice, lab tests, and surgical care. Ideally, the clinic will also have specialists either on staff or available by referral in both traditional and holistic medicine.

If you are new in town, ask for a recommendation from a friend who takes their dog's welfare seriously. Call the office and ask questions about the facilities and the veterinarian. You could even drop by and get a feel for the place yourself. Having the right veterinarian will make a great deal of difference to your peace of mind and your Corgi's well-being. You should feel comfortable calling with a problem or with a question about ongoing treatment.

Vaccines

What vaccines dogs need and how often they need them has been a subject of controversy for several years. Researchers, health care professionals, vaccine manufacturers, and dog owners do not always agree on which vaccines each dog needs or how often booster shots must be given.

In 2006, the American Animal Hospital Association issued a set of vaccination guidelines and recommendations intended to help dog owners and veterinarians sort through much of the controversy and conflicting information. The guidelines designate four vaccines as core, or essential for every dog, because of the serious nature of the diseases and their widespread distribution. These are canine distemper virus (using a modified live virus or recombinant modified live virus vaccine), canine parvovirus (using a modified live virus vaccine), canine adenovirus-2 (using a modified live virus vaccine), and rabies (using a killed virus). The general recommendations for their administration (except rabies, for which you must follow local laws) are:

- Vaccinate puppies at 6–8 weeks, 9–11 weeks, and 12–14 weeks.
- Give an initial "adult" vaccination when the dog is older than 16 weeks; two doses, three to four weeks apart, are advised, but one dose is considered protective and acceptable.

Internal Parasites

Internal parasites live in your dog's intestines or heart and lungs. They drain nutrients, can make your Corgi anemic, or even kill her in the case of a bad infestation. A fecal or blood sample examined under a microscope can reveal the presence of internal parasites. Many internal parasites are controlled by either heartworm medications or topical flea and tick treatments.

- Give a booster shot when the dog is 1 year old.
- Give a subsequent booster shot every three years, unless there are risk factors that make it necessary to vaccinate more or less often.

Noncore vaccines should only be considered for those dogs who risk exposure to a particular disease because of geographic area, lifestyle, frequency of travel, or other issues. They include vaccines against distemper-measles virus, canine parainfluenza virus, leptospirosis, Bordetella bronchiseptica, and Borrelia burgdorferi (Lyme disease).

Vaccines that are not generally recommended because the disease poses little risk to dogs or is easily treatable, or the vaccine has not been proven to be effective, are those against giardia, canine coronavirus, and canine adenovirus-1.

Often, combination injections are given to puppies, with one shot containing several core and noncore vaccines. Your veterinarian may be reluctant to use separate shots that do not include the noncore vaccines, because they must be specially ordered. If you are concerned about these noncore vaccines, talk to your vet.

Roundworms (Ascarids)

Roundworms are intestinal parasites that are common in dogs, especially puppies. Puppies can even be infected in utero. Puppies and adults alike can easily become infected from soil contaminated by roundworm eggs.

It's important to pick up your dog's stool daily to control all types of worms. When walking your dog in public areas, beware of what others leave behind.

The signs of a wormy puppy are a dry, lackluster coat, a potbelly, and a thin neck. Sometimes a puppy will cough up a worm, or one may appear in watery

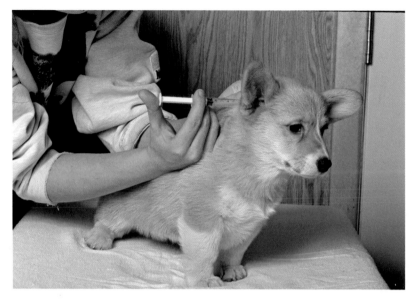

Vaccinations are an important way you can protect your dog's health.

stools. Multiple dewormings may be required. It is very important to treat them thoroughly, because roundworms present a serious public health hazard.

Hookworms

Hookworms latch onto the wall of the small intestines and suck blood. Puppies can acquire hookworms from the dam in utero, and from eggs passed in the feces. A chronic infestation causes bloody diarrhea, anemia, and weight loss. Most medications that control roundworms will kill hookworms as well. Hookworms also present a public health hazard.

Whipworms

Adult whipworms are two to three inches long with a thick and thin appearance (resembling a whip), although you are not likely to see them. They live in the large intestines, and because they lay few eggs, their presence is sometimes difficult to detect in a stool sample. Bloody diarrhea, poor coat, and weight loss are signs of whipworm infection. As with other intestinal parasites, whipworm eggs contaminate the soil.

Tapeworms

Tapeworms are a flat, segmented worm that can grow to several feet. They are usually detected when small segments break off and appear around the dog's rectum. Fresh, moist pieces wiggle, and dried ones look just like uncooked rice.

Fleas and mice are intermediary hosts for tapeworms. If your Corgi swallows a flea or hunts small rodents, chances are she will eventually get tapeworms. Your veterinarian can give her effective medication. Unfortunately, if fleas continue to flourish, or your Corgi continues to hunt, the dog can become reinfested with tapeworms, too. (See chapter 7 for information about flea control.)

Worms are especially tough in puppies, who cannot handle a heavy parasite load. Some types of parasites can also pass from your dog to you.

Heartworms

These are the most dangerous of all internal parasites. The long, thin adult worms lodge in the heart and lungs. If untreated, heartworms lead to heart failure and death. They are transmitted by an intermediary host, the mosquito. Heartworm infection is common anywhere mosquitoes live.

Prevention is far easier than treatment. If no microfilaria (larval worms) appear in a blood sample, the dog can be put on a daily or monthly heartworm preventive. Caught in the early stages, heartworms can be eradicated with relative safety.

You need to discuss the various heartworm medications and dosing schedules with your veterinarian, because these vary in different parts of the country.

Giardia

Giardia is a protozoa that causes diarrhea tinged with blood and general poor health. It is commonly acquired by drinking infected water from lakes and streams. It is also associated with poorly cleaned kennels. Puppies are particularly susceptible to contracting giardia. The problem is identified through a microscopic fecal examination. A short course of the appropriate medication will eradicate it.

Problems That Affect Corgis

As healthy as they are as a breed, there are a few medical conditions that occur with some frequency in Pembroke Welsh Corgis. Good breeders carefully screen and test their dogs for all known genetic problems before breeding them. Unfortunately, unwanted problems can pop up in even the best Corgi lines. Hopefully, you will never encounter any of the following problems. But you should be aware of what they are and some of their symptoms. Remember, though, the Corgi is generally a hardy, healthy little dog.

Back Trouble

Nestled between each vertebra of the spine is a spongy disc. If the disc ruptures, the interior material extrudes and presses against the spinal cord, causing pain and/or paralysis of the hind limbs. Early signs of disc trouble include a reluctance to stand up or to climb stairs, and a head-down posture. As the disability progresses, lack of coordination will become apparent. Any Corgi exhibiting these signs should be examined by a veterinarian and have her activities totally restricted—leash walks only and with a harness rather than a collar.

Treatment depends on the severity of the problem. Minor cases can be completely healed with crate rest and anti-inflammatory medication. These have also

The Corgi's long back can make him susceptible to spinal disc problems.

been treated very successfully with acupuncture. The more rare, severe case might respond to surgery aimed at relieving pressure on the spinal cord, along with follow-up rehabilitation.

Corgis should not be encouraged to jump down from great heights such as the couch or a bed. Keeping your Corgi fit and trim will minimize the risk of back problems.

Degenerative Myelopathy

This disease may at first appear similar to the spinal disc problem seen in Corgis, but the problem comes on gradually, not suddenly. Dogs with degenerative myelopathy have a degeneration of the nerves in the spinal cord, which moves forward from the rear. This is a problem of older dogs.

Luckily, it is not painful. But affected Corgis progress from a slight foot drag or wobbliness in the rear to being unable to walk at all. Medical care can slow progression but not totally stop or cure this problem. Recent research has identified the causative gene, and a DNA test should be available very soon.

Eye Disorders

Genetic eye abnormalities include progressive retinal atrophy (PRA), juvenile cataracts, persistent pupillary membranes (PPM), and retinal folds. The worst of these is PRA, which causes total blindness at an early age in many breeds. Fortunately, it is almost nonexistent in Pembroke Welsh Corgis.

The other three abnormalities are not disastrous and seldom cause sight impairment. Nonetheless, as these problems are of genetic origin, it is wise to test for them. The Canine Eye Registration Foundation (CERF) certifies dogs who have been examined by members of the American College of Veterinary Ophthalmologists and are free of these problems. Any Corgi used for breeding should have a current (within one year) eye certification.

Hip Dysplasia

Hip dysplasia occurs when the head of the femur (leg bone) does not fit snugly into the hip socket, and the bones are therefore worn down. It can be painful and lead to obvious lameness. Hip dysplasia is caused by complex interaction of genetics and environmental influences during puppyhood.

The condition of the hip joint can be revealed by taking special X-rays and other procedures that measure the relative laxity of the joint. The Orthopedic Foundation for Animals (OFA) is an organization that reads X-rays of dogs over 2 years old and assigns a grade ranging from clear to severely dysplastic. PennHIP is another hip-screening organization that uses a series of specially

Eye and hip problems have a genetic component. Dogs from reputable breeders will be tested for these problems before they are bred.

done X-rays to look for joint laxity. Dogs used for breeding should have an OFA certification or be screened by PennHIP.

Breeding hip dysplasia out of a line is not easy. Dysplastic puppies can appear in litters with two clear parents, and mildly dysplastic parents can produce clear puppies. Still, it is worthwhile to try everything to eliminate this debilitating disease. Corgis should be evaluated for hip dysplasia before being bred.

Von Willebrand's Disease

Von Willebrand's disease, a bleeding disorder that inhibits clotting, was first recognized in Pembroke Welsh Corgis in the 1970s. Dogs who are genetically clear of the disease and are bred to other clear dogs produce only clear offspring. However, a dog may carry the gene causing von Willebrand's disease and have no clinical signs. A carrier bred to a carrier can produce affected puppies.

The worst scenario, obviously, is a dog who bleeds to death. Because of complicated genetics, however, the disease is not always fully expressed. Abnormal thyroid function seems to be involved in the equation as well. There is currently a DNA test that should be used on all breeding animals.

Why Spay and Neuter?

Breeding dogs is a serious undertaking that should only be part of a well-planned breeding program. Why? Because dogs pass on their physical and behavioral problems to their offspring. Even healthy, well-behaved dogs can pass on problems in their genes.

Is your dog so sweet that you'd like to have a litter of puppies just like her? If you breed her to another dog, the pups will not have the same genetic heritage she has. Breeding her *parents* again will increase the odds of a similar pup, but even then, the puppies in the second litter could inherit different genes. In fact, *there is no way to breed a dog to be just like another dog.*

Meanwhile, thousands and thousands of dogs are killed in animal shelters every year simply because they have no homes. Casual breeding is a big contributor to this problem.

If you don't plan to breed your dog, is it still a good idea to spay her or neuter him? Yes!

When you spay your female:

- You avoid her heat cycles, during which she discharges blood and scent.
- It greatly reduces the risk of mammary cancer and eliminates the risk of pyometra (an often fatal infection of the uterus) and uterine cancer.
- It prevents unwanted pregnancies.
- It reduces dominance behaviors and aggression.

When you neuter your male:

- It curbs the desire to roam and to fight with other males.
- It reduces the risk of prostate problems and eliminates the risk of testicular cancer.
- It helps reduce leg lifting and mounting behavior.
- It reduces dominance behaviors and aggression.

When to Call the Veterinarian

Go to the vet right away or take your dog to an emergency veterinary clinic if:

- Your dog is choking
- Your dog is having trouble breathing
- Your dog has been injured and you cannot stop the bleeding within a few minutes
- Your dog has been stung or bitten by an insect and the site is swelling
- Your dog has been bitten by a snake
- Your dog has been bitten by another animal (including a dog) and shows any swelling or bleeding
- Your dog has touched, licked, or in any way been exposed to poison
- Your dog has been burned by either heat or caustic chemicals
- Your dog has been hit by a car
- Your dog has any obvious broken bones or cannot put any weight on one of her limbs
- Your dog has a seizure

Make an appointment to see the vet as soon as possible if:

- Your dog has been bitten by a cat, another dog, or a wild animal
- Your dog has been injured and is still limping an hour later

When Your Corgi Seems Sick

Corgis, with their expressive faces and eloquent body language, easily communicate how they feel. It then becomes your job to figure out what is wrong. If your Corgi is acting "off" in any way, you need to evaluate her carefully.

Make a list of your findings and any unusual circumstances before you call your veterinarian. All these observations will help determine what the problem is. Corgis are smart, but they cannot talk. The more information you can provide, the easier it will be for your veterinarian to treat your dog.

- Your dog has unexplained swelling or redness
- Your dog's appetite changes
- Your dog vomits repeatedly and can't seem to keep food down, or drools excessively while eating
- You see any changes in your dog's urination or defecation (pain during elimination, change in regular habits, blood in urine or stool, diarrhea, foul-smelling stool)
- Your dog scoots her rear end on the floor
- Your dog's energy level, attitude, or behavior changes for no apparent reason
- Your dog has crusty or cloudy eyes, or excessive tearing or discharge
- Your dog's nose is dry or chapped, hot, crusty, or runny
- Your dog's ears smell foul, have a dark discharge, or seem excessively waxy
- Your dog's gums are inflamed or bleeding, her teeth look brown, or her breath is foul
- Your dog's skin is red, flaky, itchy, or inflamed, or she keeps chewing at certain spots
- Your dog's coat is dull, dry, brittle, or bare in spots
- Your dog's paws are red, swollen, tender, cracked, or the nails are split or too long
- Your dog is panting excessively, wheezing, unable to catch her breath, breathing heavily, or sounds strange when she breathes

Emergencies and First Aid

There are times when you have to act at once, even before you can get emergency veterinary care. Perhaps you are not at home, or the clinic is closed and the emergency facility is far away. Or your dog will require first aid in order to prevent a situation from escalating while you transport her to the veterinarian.

There are a few handy first-aid techniques you should know. But first, if at all possible, call your veterinarian or the emergency clinic. Make sure the phone numbers are easy to find and that you have clear directions.

Animal Bites

Puncture wounds from animal bites can become infected. The teeth carry bacteria into the flesh and sometimes the small opening heals over, trapping pathogens inside. Trim the hair away from the bite site and rinse the wound with sterile saline or water. Apply an antiseptic ointment. Keep the wound open until it heals from within. If swelling occurs, take your dog to the veterinarian.

If the wound is large, deep, or a tear, place gauze or a clean cloth over the wound and apply pressure to control the bleeding. Then call your veterinarian.

Choking

If the dog is drooling, pawing her jaws, or gasping, look into her mouth. You may need to use a flashlight. If you can see something blocking the throat, try to get it out at once with your fingers, tweezers, or even pliers.

If it won't move, try a doggy Heimlich maneuver. Being careful not to damage the ribs, press sharply behind the ribs with the palms of your hands. This can be done with the dog either standing or lying on her side. If you cannot remove the object, rush to the veterinary clinic.

It's important to know what's normal for your dog. Then you will also know when she's not feeling quite right.

On a warm day, Corgis, with their thick coats, can quickly become overheated.

Fractures and Other Traumas

When a dog suffers a fracture or trauma, a muzzle is necessary. Move the injured area as little as possible while transporting the dog to the veterinarian.

If a leg appears to be broken, try to immobilize it using a short piece of wood or stiff cardboard, padded and tied on with gauze or tape. If there has been a car accident, make a stretcher from a board to keep the dog from moving and adding to the damage. If she is quite still and her gums are white, she probably is in shock. Cover her to retain warmth, keep her head a bit lower than her body, and go directly to the nearest veterinary clinic.

> **TIP**
>
> When a dog is frightened and in pain, she may snap as you try to help her. The safest thing to do is make a temporary muzzle. Knot a piece of gauze or old stocking leg around the top of her muzzle, down under the chin, and then behind the ears. She will be able to breathe, because the cartilage in her nose keeps it from getting too tight.

Heatstroke

It's amazing how many dogs are left to perish in unventilated cars each summer. *Never* leave your Corgi unattended in a car, even with the windows open. Cars become death traps in a matter of minutes.

If she becomes overheated, has difficulty breathing, pants rapidly, or begins to stagger, act at once. Get her into cool water or put cold compresses on her groin area. Check her temperature and seek the help of a veterinarian.

Insect Sting

Remove the stinger if possible with tweezers, apply a paste of baking soda to the site, and watch carefully. Some dogs will have an allergic reaction, and the eyelids and muzzle begin to swell. If you see these signs, call the veterinarian immediately. A severe reaction may be life-threatening.

Poisoning

Dogs, especially puppies, eat all sorts of things they shouldn't. Some poisonous items are listed in chapter 5. Warfarin, slug bait, and antifreeze top the list of common poisons. If you suspect your dog has eaten poison, take action immediately. Do not wait for signs to develop.

ASPCA Animal Poison Control Center

The ASPCA Animal Poison Control Center has a staff of licensed veterinarians and board-certified toxicologists available 24 hours a day, 365 days a year. The number to call is (888) 426-4435. You will be charged a consultation fee of $60 per case, charged to most major credit cards. There is no charge for follow-up calls in critical cases. At your request, they will also contact your veterinarian. Specific treatment and information can be provided via fax.

Keep the poison control number in large, legible print with your other emergency telephone numbers. When you call, be prepared to give your name, address, and phone number; what your dog has gotten into (the amount and how long ago); your dog's breed, age, sex, and weight; and what signs and symptoms the dog is showing. You can log onto www.aspca.org and click on "Animal Poison Control Center" for more information, including a list of toxic and nontoxic plants.

How to Make a Canine First-Aid Kit

If your dog hurts herself, even a minor cut, it can be very upsetting for both of you. Having a first-aid kit handy will help you to help her, calmly and efficiently. What should be in your canine first-aid kit?

- Antibiotic ointment
- Antiseptic and antibacterial cleansing wipes
- Benadryl
- Cotton-tipped applicators
- Disposable razor
- Elastic wrap bandages
- Extra leash and collar
- First-aid tape of various widths
- Gauze bandage roll
- Gauze pads of different sizes, including eye pads
- Hydrogen peroxide
- Instant cold compress
- Kaopectate or Pepto-Bismol tablets or liquid
- Latex gloves
- Lubricating jelly
- Muzzle
- Nail clippers
- Pen, pencil, and paper for notes and directions
- Plastic syringe with no needle (for administering liquids)
- Round-ended scissors and pointy scissors
- Safety pins
- Sterile saline eyewash
- Thermometer (rectal)
- Tweezers

The first thing to do is find out what has been ingested. Then call your veterinarian or the ASPCA Animal Poison Control Center hotline (see the box on page 98). Let the trained personnel tell you whether to induce vomiting and how to do so. For some types of poisoning, inducing vomiting is *not* appropriate.

Part III
Enjoying Your Corgi

Chapter 9

Training Your Pembroke Welsh Corgi

by Peggy Moran

Training makes your best friend better! A properly trained dog has a happier life and a longer life expectancy. He is also more appreciated by the people he encounters each day, both at home and out and about.

A trained dog walks nicely and joins his family often, going places untrained dogs cannot go. He is never rude or unruly, and he always happily comes when called. When he meets people for the first time, he greets them by sitting and waiting to be petted, rather than jumping up. At home he doesn't compete with his human family, and alone he is not destructive or overly anxious. He isn't continually nagged with words like "no," since he has learned not to misbehave in the first place. He is never shamed, harshly punished, or treated unkindly, and he is a well-loved, involved member of the family.

Sounds good, doesn't it? If you are willing to invest some time, thought, and patience, the words above could soon be used to describe your dog (though perhaps changing "he" to "she"). Educating your pet in a positive way is fun and easy, and there is no better gift you can give your pet than the guarantee of improved understanding and a great relationship.

This chapter will explain how to offer kind leadership, reshape your pet's behavior in a positive and practical way, and even get a head start on simple obedience training.

Understanding Builds the Bond

Dog training is a learning adventure on both ends of the leash. Before attempting to teach their dog new behaviors or change unwanted ones, thoughtful dog owners take the time to understand why their pets behave the way they do, and how their own behavior can be either a positive or negative influence on their dog.

Canine Nature

Loving dogs as much as we do, it's easy to forget they are a completely different species. Despite sharing our homes and living as appreciated members of our families, dogs do not think or learn exactly the same way people do. Even if you love your dog like a child, you must remember to respect the fact that he is actually a dog.

Dogs have no idea when their behavior is inappropriate from a human perspective. They are not aware of the value of possessions they chew or of messes they make or the worry they sometimes seem to cause. While people tend to look at behavior as good and bad or right and wrong, dogs just discover what works and what doesn't work. Then they behave accordingly, learning from their own experiences and increasing or reducing behaviors to improve results for themselves.

You might wonder, "But don't dogs want to please us?" My answer is yes, provided your pleasure reflects back to them in positive ways they can feel and appreciate. Dogs do things for *dog* reasons, and everything they do works for them in some way or they wouldn't be doing it!

The Social Dog

Our pets descended from animals who lived in tightly knit, cooperative social groups. Though far removed in appearance and lifestyle from their ancestors, our dogs still relate in many of the same ways their wild relatives did. And in their relationships with one another, wild canids either lead or follow.

Canine ranking relationships are not about cruelty and power; they are about achievement and abilities. Competent dogs with high levels of drive and confidence step up, while deferring dogs step aside. But followers don't get the short end of the stick; they benefit from the security of having a more competent dog at the helm.

Our domestic dogs still measure themselves against other members of their group—us! Dog owners whose actions lead to positive results have willing, secure followers. But dogs may step up and fill the void or cut loose and do their own thing when their people fail to show capable leadership. When dogs are pushy, aggressive, and rude, or independent and unwilling, it's not because they have designs on the role of "master." It is more likely their owners failed to provide consistent leadership.

Dogs in training benefit from their handler's good leadership. Their education flows smoothly because they are impressed. Being in charge doesn't require you to physically dominate or punish your dog. You simply need to make some subtle changes in the way you relate to him every day.

Lead Your Pack!

Create schedules and structure daily activities. Dogs are creatures of habit and routines will create security. Feed meals at the same times each day and also try to schedule regular walks, training practices, and toilet outings. Your predictability will help your dog be patient.

Ask your dog to perform a task. Before releasing him to food or freedom, have him do something as simple as sit on command. Teach him that cooperation earns great results!

Give a release prompt (such as "let's go") when going through doors leading outside. This is a better idea than allowing your impatient pup to rush past you.

Pet your dog when he is calm, not when he is excited. Turn your touch into a tool that relaxes and settles.

Reward desirable rather than inappropriate behavior. Petting a jumping dog (who hasn't been invited up) reinforces jumping. Pet sitting dogs, and only invite lap dogs up after they've first "asked" by waiting for your invitation.

Replace personal punishment with positive reinforcement. Show a dog what *to do,* and motivate him to want to do it, and there will be no need to punish him for what he should *not do.* Dogs naturally follow, without the need for force or harshness.

Play creatively and appropriately. Your dog will learn the most about his social rank when he is playing with you. During play, dogs work to control toys and try to get the best of one another in a friendly way. The wrong sorts of play can create problems: For example, tug of war can lead to aggressiveness. Allowing your dog to control toys during play may result in possessive guarding when he has something he really values, such as a bone. Dogs who are chased during play may later run away from you when you approach to leash them. The right kinds of play will help increase your dog's social confidence while you gently assert your leadership.

How Dogs Learn (and How They Don't)

Dog training begins as a meeting of minds—yours and your dog's. Though the end goal may be to get your dog's body to behave in a specific way, training starts as a mind game. Your dog is learning all the time by observing the consequences of his actions and social interactions. He is always seeking out what he perceives as desirable and trying to avoid what he perceives as undesirable.

He will naturally repeat a behavior that either brings him more good stuff or makes bad stuff go away (these are both types of reinforcement). He will naturally avoid a behavior that brings him more bad stuff or makes the good stuff go away (these are both types of punishment).

Both reinforcement and punishment can be perceived as either the direct result of something the dog did himself, or as coming from an outside source.

Using Life's Rewards

Your best friend is smart and he is also cooperative. When the best things in life can only be had by working with you, your dog will view you as a facilitator. You unlock doors to all of the positively reinforcing experiences he values: his freedom, his friends at the park, food, affection, walks, and play. The trained dog accompanies you through those doors and waits to see what working with you will bring.

Rewarding your dog for good behavior is called positive reinforcement, and, as we've just seen, it increases the likelihood that he will repeat that behavior. The perfect reward is anything your dog wants that is safe and appropriate. Don't limit yourself to toys, treats, and things that come directly from you. Harness life's positives—barking at squirrels, chasing a falling leaf, bounding away from you at the dog park, pausing for a moment to sniff everything—and allow your dog to earn access to those things as rewards that come from cooperating with you. When he looks at you, when he sits, when he comes when you call—any prompted behavior can earn one of life's rewards. When he works with you, he earns the things he most appreciates; but when he tries to get those things on his own, he cannot. Rather than seeing you as someone who always says "no," your dog will view you as the one who says "let's go!" He will *want* to follow.

What About Punishment?

Not only is it unnecessary to personally punish dogs, it is abusive. No matter how convinced you are that your dog "knows right from wrong," in reality he will associate personal punishment with the punisher. The resulting cowering, "guilty"-looking postures are actually displays of submission and fear. Later,

Purely Positive Reinforcement

With positive training, we emphasize teaching dogs what they should do to earn reinforcements, rather than punishing them for unwanted behaviors.

- Focus on teaching "do" rather than "don't." For example, a sitting dog isn't jumping.
- Use positive reinforcers that are valuable to your dog and the situation: A tired dog values rest; a confined dog values freedom.
- Play (appropriately)!
- Be a consistent leader.
- Set your dog up for success by anticipating and preventing problems.
- Notice and reward desirable behavior, and give him lots of attention when he is being good.
- Train ethically. Use humane methods and equipment that do not frighten or hurt your dog.
- When you are angry, walk away and plan a positive strategy.
- Keep practice sessions short and sweet. Five to ten minutes, three to five times a day is best.

when the punisher isn't around and the coast is clear, the same behavior he was punished for—such as raiding a trash can—might bring a self-delivered, very tasty result. The punished dog hasn't learned not to misbehave; he has learned to not get caught.

Does punishment ever have a place in dog training? Many people will heartily insist it does not. But dog owners often get frustrated as they try to stick to the path of all-positive reinforcement. It sure sounds great, but is it realistic, or even natural, to *never* say "no" to your dog?

A wild dog's life is not *all* positive. Hunger and thirst are both examples of negative reinforcement; the resulting discomfort motivates the wild dog to seek food and water. He encounters natural aversives such as pesky insects; mats in his coat; cold days; rainy days; sweltering hot days; and occasional run-ins with thorns, brambles, skunks, bees, and other nastiness. These all affect his behavior, as he tries to avoid the bad stuff whenever possible. The wild dog also occasionally encounters social punishers from others in his group when he gets too pushy. Starting with a growl or a snap from Mom, and later some mild and ritualized discipline from other members of his four-legged family, he learns to modify behaviors that elicit grouchy responses.

Our pet dogs don't naturally experience all positive results either, because they learn from their surroundings and from social experiences with other dogs. Watch a group of pet dogs playing together and you'll see a very old educational system still being used. As they wrestle and attempt to assert themselves, you'll notice many mouth-on-neck moments. Their playful biting is inhibited, with no intention to cause harm, but their message is clear: "Say uncle or this could hurt more!"

Observing that punishment does occur in nature, some people may feel compelled to try to be like the big wolf with their pet dogs. Becoming aggressive or heavy-handed with your pet will backfire! Your dog will not be impressed, nor will he want to follow you. Punishment causes dogs to change their behavior to avoid or escape discomfort and threats. Threatened dogs will either become very passive and offer submissive, appeasing postures, attempt to flee, or rise to the occasion and fight back. When people personally punish their dogs in an angry manner, one of these three defensive mechanisms will be triggered. Which one depends on a dog's genetic temperament as well as his past social experiences. Since we don't want to make our pets feel the need to avoid or escape us, personal punishment has no place in our training.

Remote Consequences

Sometimes, however, all-positive reinforcement is just not enough. That's because not all reinforcement comes from us. An inappropriate behavior can be self-reinforcing—just doing it makes the dog feel better in some way, whether you are there to say "good boy!" or not. Some examples are eating garbage, pulling the stuffing out of your sofa, barking at passersby, or urinating on the floor.

Although you don't want to personally punish your dog, the occasional deterrent may be called for to help derail these kinds of self-rewarding misbehaviors. In these cases, mild forms of impersonal or remote punishment can be used as part of a correction. The goal isn't to make your dog feel bad or to "know he has done wrong," but to help redirect him to alternate behaviors that are more acceptable to you.

The Problems with Personal Punishment

- Personally punished dogs are not taught appropriate behaviors.
- Personally punished dogs only stop misbehaving when they are caught or interrupted, but they don't learn not to misbehave when they are alone.
- Personally punished dogs become shy, fearful, and distrusting.
- Personally punished dogs may become defensively aggressive.
- Personally punished dogs become suppressed and inhibited.
- Personally punished dogs become stressed, triggering stress-reducing behaviors that their owners interpret as acts of spite, triggering even more punishment.
- Personally punished dogs have stressed owners.
- Personally punished dogs may begin to repeat behaviors they have been taught will result in negative, but predictable, attention.
- Personally punished dogs are more likely to be given away than are positively trained dogs.

You do this by pairing a slightly startling, totally impersonal sound with an equally impersonal and *very mild* remote consequence. The impersonal sound might be a single shake of an empty plastic pop bottle with pennies in it, held out of your dog's sight. Or you could use a vocal expression such as "eh!" delivered with you looking *away* from your misbehaving dog.

Pair your chosen sound—the penny bottle or "eh!"—with either a slight tug on his collar or a sneaky spritz on the rump from a water bottle. Do this right *as* he touches something he should not; bad timing will confuse your dog and undermine your training success.

To keep things under your control and make sure you get the timing right, it's best to do this as a setup. "Accidentally" drop a shoe on the floor, and then help your dog learn some things are best avoided. As he sniffs the shoe say "eh!" without looking at him and give a *slight* tug against his collar. This sound will quickly become meaningful as a correction all by itself—sometimes after just one setup—making the tug correction obsolete. The tug lets your dog see that you were right; going for that shoe *was* a bad idea! Your wise dog will be more likely to heed your warning next time, and probably move closer to you where it's safe. Be a good friend and pick up the nasty shoe. He'll be relieved and you'll look heroic. Later, when he's home alone and encounters a stray shoe, he'll want to give it a wide berth.

Your negative marking sound will come in handy in the future, when your dog begins to venture down the wrong behavioral path. The goal is not to announce your disapproval or to threaten your dog. You are not telling him to stop or showing how *you* feel about his behavior. You are sounding a warning to a friend who's venturing off toward danger—"I wouldn't if I were you!" Suddenly, there is an abrupt, rather startling, noise! Now is the moment to redirect him and help him earn positive reinforcement. That interrupted behavior will become something he wants to avoid in the future, but he won't want to avoid you.

Practical Commands for Family Pets

Before you begin training your dog, let's look at some equipment you'll want to have on hand:

- **A buckle collar** is fine for most dogs. If your dog pulls *very* hard, try a head collar, a device similar to a horse halter that helps reduce pulling by turning the dog's head. *Do not* use a choke chain (sometimes called a training collar), because they cause physical harm even when used correctly.
- **Six-foot training leash and twenty-six–foot retractable leash.**
- **A few empty plastic soda bottles with about twenty pennies in each one.** This will be used to impersonally interrupt misbehaviors before redirecting dogs to more positive activities.
- **A favorite squeaky toy,** to motivate, attract attention, and reward your dog during training.

Lure your dog to take just a few steps with you on the leash by being inviting and enthusiastic. Make sure you reward him for his efforts.

Baby Steps

Allow your young pup to drag a short, lightweight leash attached to a buckle collar for a few *supervised* moments, several times each day. At first the leash may annoy him and he may jump around a bit trying to get away from it. Distract him with your squeaky toy or a bit of his kibble and he'll quickly get used to his new "tail."

Begin walking him on the leash by holding the end and following him. As he adapts, you can begin to assert gentle direct pressure to teach him to follow you. Don't jerk or yank, or he will become afraid to walk when the leash is on. If he becomes hesitant, squat down facing him and let him figure out that by moving toward you he is safe and secure. If he remains confused or frightened and doesn't come to you, go to him and help him understand that you provide safe harbor while he's on the leash. Then back away a few steps and try again to lure him to you. As he learns that you are the "home base," he'll want to follow when you walk a few steps, waiting for you to stop, squat down, and make him feel great.

So Attached to You!

The next step in training your dog—and this is a very important one—is to begin spending at least an hour or more each day with him on a four- to six-foot leash, held by or tethered to you. This training will increase his attachment to you—literally!—as you sit quietly or walk about, tending to your household business. When you are quiet, he'll learn it is time to settle; when you are active, he'll learn to move with you. Tethering also keeps him out of trouble when you are busy but still want his company. It is a great alternative to confining a dog, and can be used instead of crating any time you're home and need to slow him down a bit.

Rotating your dog from supervised freedom to tethered time to some quiet time in the crate or his gated area gives him a diverse and balanced day while he is learning. Two confined or tethered hours is the most you should require of your dog in one stretch, before changing to some supervised freedom, play, or a walk.

The dog in training may, at times, be stressed by all of the changes he is dealing with. Provide a stress outlet, such as a toy to chew on, when he is confined or tethered. He will settle into his quiet time more quickly and completely. Always be sure to provide several rounds of daily play and free time (in a fenced area or on your retractable leash) in addition to plenty of chewing materials.

Dog Talk

Dogs don't speak in words, but they do have a language—body language. They use postures, vocalizations, movements, facial gestures, odors, and touch—usually with their mouths—to communicate what they are feeling and thinking.

Tethering your dog is great way to keep him calm and under control, but still with you.

We also "speak" using body language. We have quite an array of postures, movements, and facial gestures that accompany our touch and language as we attempt to communicate with our pets. And our dogs can quickly figure us out!

Alone, without associations, words are just noises. But, because we pair them with meaningful body language, our dogs make the connection. Dogs can really learn to understand much of what we *say*, if what we *do* at the same time is consistent.

The Positive Marker

Start your dog's education with one of the best tricks in dog training: Pair various positive reinforcers—food, a toy, touch—with a sound such as a click on a clicker (which you can get at the pet supply store) or a spoken word like "good!" or "yes!" This will enable you to later "mark" your dog's desirable behaviors.

It seems too easy: Just say "yes!" and give the dog his toy. (Or use whatever sound and reward you have chosen.) Later, when you make your marking sound right at the instant your dog does the right thing, he will know you are going to be giving him something good for that particular action. And he'll be eager to repeat the behavior to hear you mark it again!

Next, you must teach your dog to understand the meaning of cues you'll be using to ask him to perform specific behaviors. This is easy, too. Does he already do things you might like him to do on command? Of course! He lies down, he sits, he picks things up, he drops them again, he comes to you. All of the behaviors you'd like to control are already part of your dog's natural repertoire. The trick is getting him to offer those behaviors when you ask for them. And that means you have to teach him to associate a particular behavior on his part with a particular behavior on your part.

Sit Happens

Teach your dog an important new rule: From now on, he is only touched and petted when he is either sitting or lying down. You won't need to ask him to sit; in fact, you should not. Just keeping him tethered near you so there isn't much to do but stand, be ignored, or settle, and wait until sit happens.

He may pester you a bit, but be stoic and unresponsive. Starting now, when *you* are sitting down, a sitting dog is the only one you see and pay attention to. He will eventually sit, and as he does, attach the word "sit"—but don't be too excited or he'll jump right back up. Now mark with your positive sound that promises something good, then reward him with a slow, quiet, settling pet.

Training requires consistent reinforcement. Ask others to also wait until your dog is sitting and calm to touch him, and he will associate being petted with being relaxed. Be sure you train your dog to associate everyone's touch with quiet bonding.

Reinforcing "Sit" as a Command

Since your dog now understands one concept of working for a living—sit to earn petting—you can begin to shape and reinforce his desire to sit. Hold toys, treats, his bowl of food, and turn into a statue. But don't prompt him to sit! Instead, remain frozen and unavailable, looking somewhere out into space, over his head. He will put on a bit of a show, trying to get a response from you, and may offer various behaviors, but only one will push your button—sitting. Wait for him to offer the "right" behavior, and when he does, you unfreeze. Say "sit," then mark with an excited "good!" and give him the toy or treat with a release command—"OK!"

When you notice spontaneous sits occurring, be sure to take advantage of those free opportunities to make your command sequence meaningful and positive. Say "sit" as you observe sit happen—then mark with "good!" and praise, pet, or reward the dog. Soon, every time you look at your dog he'll be sitting and looking right back at you!

Now, after thirty days of purely positive practice, it's time to give him a test. When he is just walking around doing his own thing, suddenly ask him to sit. He'll probably do it right away. If he doesn't, do *not* repeat your command, or you'll just undermine its meaning ("sit" means sit *now;* the command is not "sit, sit, sit, sit"). Instead, get something he likes and let him know you have it. Wait for him to offer the sit—he will—then say "sit!" and complete your marking and rewarding sequence.

OK

"OK" will probably rate as one of your dog's favorite words. It's like the word "recess" to schoolchildren. It is the word used to release your dog from a command. You can introduce "OK" during your "sit" practice. When he gets up from a sit, say "OK" to tell him the sitting is finished. Soon that sound will mean "freedom."

Make it even more meaningful and positive. Whenever he spontaneously bounds away, say "OK!" Squeak a toy, and when he notices and shows interest, toss it for him.

Down

I've mentioned that you should only pet your dog when he is either sitting or lying down. Now, using the approach I've just introduced for "sit," teach your dog to lie down. You will be a statue, and hold something he would like to get but that you'll only release to a dog who is lying down. It helps to lower the desired item to the floor in front of him, still not speaking and not letting him have it until he offers you the new behavior you are seeking.

Lower your dog's reward to the floor to help him figure out what behavior will earn him his reward.

He may offer a sit and then wait expectantly, but you must make him keep searching for the new trick that triggers your generosity. Allow your dog to experiment and find the right answer, even if he has to search around for it first. When he lands on "down" and learns it is another behavior that works, he'll offer it more quickly the next time.

Don't say "down" until he lies down, to tightly associate your prompt with the correct behavior. To say "down, down, down" as he is sitting, looking at you, or pawing at the toy would make "down" mean those behaviors instead! Whichever behavior he offers, a training opportunity has been created. Once you've attached and shaped both sitting and lying down, you can ask for both behaviors with your verbal prompts, "sit" or "down." Be sure to only reinforce the "correct" reply!

Stay

"Stay" can easily be taught as an extension of what you've already been practicing. To teach "stay," you follow the entire sequence for reinforcing a "sit" or "down," except you wait a bit longer before you give the release word, "OK!" Wait a second or two longer during each practice before saying "OK!" and releasing your dog to the positive reinforcer (toy, treat, or one of life's other rewards).

You can step on the leash to help your dog understand the down-stay, but only do this when he is already lying down. You don't want to hurt him!

If he gets up before you've said "OK," you have two choices: pretend the release was your idea and quickly interject "OK!" as he breaks; or, if he is more experienced and practiced, mark the behavior with your correction sound— "eh!"— and then gently put him back on the spot, wait for him to lie down, and begin again. Be sure the next three practices are a success. Ask him to wait for just a second, and release him before he can be wrong. You need to keep your dog feeling like more of a success than a failure as you begin to test his training in increasingly more distracting and difficult situations.

As he gets the hang of it—he stays until you say "OK"— you can gradually push for longer times—up to a minute on a sit-stay, and up to three minutes on a down-stay. You can also gradually add distractions and work in new environments. To add a minor self-correction for the down-stay, stand on the dog's leash after he lies down, allowing about three inches of slack. If tries to get up before you've said "OK," he'll discover it doesn't work.

Do not step on the leash to make your dog lie down! This could badly hurt his neck, and will destroy his trust in you. Remember, we are teaching our dogs to make the best choices, not inflicting our answers upon them!

Come

Rather than thinking of "come" as an action—"come to me"—think of it as a place—"the dog is sitting in front of me, facing me." Since your dog by now really likes sitting to earn your touch and other positive reinforcement, he's likely to sometimes sit directly in front of you, facing you, all on his own. When this happens, give it a specific name: "come."

Now follow the rest of the training steps you have learned to make him like doing it and reinforce the behavior by practicing it any chance you get. Anything your dog wants and likes could be earned as a result of his first offering the sit-in-front known as "come."

You can help guide him into the right location. Use your hands as "landing gear" and pat the insides of your legs at his nose level. Do this while backing up a bit, to help him maneuver to the straight-in-front, facing-you position. Don't say the

Pat the insides of your legs to show your dog exactly where you like him to sit when you say "come."

word "come" while he's maneuvering, because he hasn't! You are trying to make "come" the end result, not the work in progress.

You can also help your dog by marking his movement in the right direction: Use your positive sound or word to promise he is getting warm. When he finally sits facing you, enthusiastically say "come," mark again with your positive word, and release him with an enthusiastic "OK!" Make it so worth his while, with lots of play and praise, that he can't wait for you to ask him to come again!

Building a Better Recall

Practice, practice, practice. Now, practice some more. Teach your dog that all good things in life hinge upon him first sitting in front of you in a behavior named "come." When you think he really has got it, test him by asking him to "come" as you gradually add distractions and change locations. Expect setbacks as you make these changes and practice accordingly. Lower your expectations and make his task easier so he is able to get it right. Use those distractions as rewards, when they are appropriate. For example, let him check out the interesting leaf that blew by as a reward for first coming to you and ignoring it.

Add distance and call your dog to come while he is on his retractable leash. If he refuses and sits looking at you blankly, *do not* jerk, tug, "pop," or reel him in. Do nothing! It is his move; wait to see what behavior he offers. He'll either begin to approach (mark the behavior with an excited "good!"), sit and do nothing (just keep waiting), or he'll try to move in some direction other than toward you. If he tries to leave, use your correction marker—"eh!"— and bring him to a stop by letting him walk to the end of the leash, *not* by jerking him. Now walk to him in a neutral manner, and don't jerk or show any disapproval. Gently bring him back to the spot where he was when you called him, then back away and face him, still waiting and not reissuing your command. Let him keep examining his options until he finds the one that works—yours!

If you have practiced everything I've suggested so far and given your dog a chance to really learn what "come" means, he is well aware of what you want and is quite intelligently weighing all his options. The only way he'll know your way is the one that works is to be allowed to examine his other choices and discover that they *don't* work.

Sooner or later every dog tests his training. Don't be offended or angry when your dog tests you. No matter how positive you've made it, he won't always want to do everything you ask, every time. When he explores the "what happens if I don't" scenario, your training is being strengthened. He will discover through his own process of trial and error that the best—and only—way out of a command he really doesn't feel compelled to obey is to obey it.

Let's Go

Many pet owners wonder if they can retain control while walking their dogs and still allow at least some running in front, sniffing, and playing. You might worry that allowing your dog occasional freedom could result in him expecting it all the time, leading to a testy, leash-straining walk. It's possible for both parties on the leash to have an enjoyable experience by implementing and reinforcing well-thought-out training techniques.

Begin by making word associations you'll use on your walks. Give the dog some slack on the leash, and as he starts to walk away from you say "OK" and begin to follow him.

Do not let him drag you; set the pace even when he is being given a turn at being the leader. Whenever he starts to pull, just come to a standstill and refuse to move (or refuse to allow him to continue forward) until there is slack in the leash. Do this correction without saying anything at all. When he isn't pulling, you may decide to just stand still and let him sniff about within the range the slack leash allows, or you may even mosey along following him. After a few minutes of "recess," it is time to work. Say something like "that's it" or "time's up," close the distance between you and your dog, and touch him.

Next say "let's go" (or whatever command you want to use to mean "follow me as we walk"). Turn and walk off, and, if he follows, mark his behavior with "good!" Then stop,

Give your dog slack on his leash as you walk and let him make the decision to walk with you.

When your dog catches up with you, make sure you let him know what a great dog he is!

Intersperse periods of attentive walking, where your dog is on a shorter leash, with periods on a slack leash, where he is allowed to look and sniff around.

squat down, and let him catch you. Make him glad he did! Start again, and do a few transitions as he gets the hang of your follow-the-leader game, speeding up, slowing down, and trying to make it fun. When you stop, he gets to catch up and receive some deserved positive reinforcement. Don't forget that's the reason he is following you, so be sure to make it worth his while!

Require him to remain attentive to you. Do not allow sniffing, playing, eliminating, or pulling during your time as leader on a walk. If he seems to get distracted—which, by the way, is the main reason dogs walk poorly with their people— change direction or pace without saying a word. Just help him realize "oops, I lost track of my human." Do not jerk his neck and say "heel"—this will make the word "heel" mean pain in the neck and will not encourage him to cooperate with you. Don't repeat "let's go," either. He needs to figure out that it is his job to keep track of and follow you if he wants to earn the positive benefits you provide.

The best reward you can give a dog for performing an attentive, controlled walk is a few minutes of walking without all of the controls. Of course, he must remain on a leash even during the "recess" parts of the walk, but allowing him to discriminate between attentive following—"let's go"—and having a few moments of relaxation—"OK"—will increase his willingness to work.

Training for Attention

Your dog pretty much has a one-track mind. Once he is focused on something, everything else is excluded. This can be great, for instance, when he's focusing on you! But it can also be dangerous if, for example, his attention is riveted on the bunny he is chasing and he does not hear you call—that is, not unless he has been trained to pay attention when you say his name.

When you call your dog's name, you will again be seeking a specific response—eye contact. The best way to teach this is to trigger his alerting response by making a noise with your mouth, such as whistling or a kissing sound, and then immediately doing something he'll find very intriguing.

You can play a treasure hunt game to help teach him to regard his name as a request for attention. As a bonus, you can reinforce the rest of his new vocabulary at the same time.

Treasure Hunt

Make a kissing sound, then jump up and find a dog toy or dramatically raid the fridge and rather noisily eat a piece of cheese. After doing this twice, make a kissing sound and then look at your dog.

Of course he is looking at you! He is waiting to see if that sound—the kissing sound—means you're going to go hunting again. After all, you're so good at it! Because he is looking, say his name, mark with "good," then go hunting and find his toy. Release it to him with an "OK." At any point if he follows you, attach your "let's go!" command; if he leaves you, give permission with "OK."

When you say your dog's name, you'll want him to make eye contact with you. Begin teaching this by making yourself so intriguing that he can't help but look.

Using this approach, he cannot be wrong—any behavior your dog offers can be named. You can add things like "take it" when he picks up a toy, and "thank you" when he happens to drop one. Many opportunities to make your new vocabulary meaningful and positive can be found within this simple training game.

Problems to watch out for when teaching the treasure hunt:

- You really do not want your dog to come to you when you call his name (later, when you try to engage his attention to ask him to stay, he'll already be on his way toward you). You just want him to look at you.
- Saying "watch me, watch me" doesn't teach your dog to *offer* his attention. It just makes you a background noise.

- Don't lure your dog's attention with the reward. Get his attention and then reward him for looking. Try holding a toy in one hand with your arm stretched out to your side. Wait until he looks at you rather than the toy. Now say his name then mark with "good!" and release the toy. As he goes for it, say "OK."

Teaching Cooperation

Never punish your dog for failing to obey you or try to punish him into compliance. Bribing, repeating yourself, and doing a behavior for him all avoid the real issue of dog training—his will. He must be helped to be willing, not made to achieve tasks. Good dog training helps your dog want to obey. He learns that he can gain what he values most through cooperation and compliance, and can't gain those things any other way.

To get your dog's attention, try holding his toy with your arm out to your side. Wait until he looks at you, then mark the moment and give him the toy.

Your dog is learning to *earn*, rather than expect, the good things in life. And you've become much more important to him than you were before. Because you are allowing him to experiment and learn, he doesn't have to be forced, manipulated, or bribed. When he wants something, he can gain it by cooperating with you. One of those "somethings"—and a great reward you shouldn't underestimate—is your positive attention, paid to him with love and sincere approval!

Chapter 10

Housetraining Your Pembroke Welsh Corgi

Excerpted from Housetraining: An Owner's Guide to a Happy Healthy Pet, 1st Edition, *by September Morn*

By the time puppies are about 3 weeks old, they start to follow their mother around. When they are a few steps away from their clean sleeping area, the mama dog stops. The pups try to nurse but mom won't allow it. The pups mill around in frustration, then nature calls and they all urinate and defecate here, away from their bed. The mother dog returns to the nest, with her brood waddling behind her. Their first housetraining lesson has been a success.

The next one to housetrain puppies should be their breeder. The breeder watches as the puppies eliminate, then deftly removes the soiled papers and replaces them with clean papers before the pups can traipse back through their messes. He has wisely arranged the puppies' space so their bed, food, and drinking water are as far away from the elimination area as possible. This way, when the pups follow their mama, they will move away from their sleeping and eating area before eliminating. This habit will help the pups be easily housetrained.

Your Housetraining Shopping List

While your puppy's mother and breeder are getting her started on good housetraining habits, you'll need to do some shopping. If you have all the essentials in place before your dog arrives, it will be easier to help her learn the rules from day one.

Newspaper: The younger your puppy and larger her breed, the more newspapers you'll need. Newspaper is absorbent, abundant, cheap, and convenient.

Puddle Pads: If you prefer not to stockpile newspaper, a commercial alternative is puddle pads. These thick paper pads can be purchased under several trade names at pet supply stores. The pads have waterproof backing, so puppy urine doesn't seep through onto the floor. Their disadvantages are that they will cost you more than newspapers and that they contain plastics that are not biodegradable.

Poop Removal Tool: There are several types of poop removal tools available. Some are designed with a separate pan and rake, and others have the handles hinged like scissors. Some scoops need two hands for operation, while others are designed for one-handed use. Try out the different brands at your pet supply store. Put a handful of pebbles or dog kibble on the floor and then pick them up with each type of scoop to determine which works best for you.

Plastic Bags: When you take your dog outside your yard, you *must* pick up after her. Dog waste is unsightly, smelly, and can harbor disease. In many cities and towns, the law mandates dog owners clean up pet waste deposited on public ground. Picking up after your dog using a plastic bag scoop is simple. Just put your hand inside the bag, like a mitten, and then grab the droppings. Turn the bag inside out, tie the top, and that's that.

Crate: To housetrain a puppy, you will need some way to confine her when you're unable to supervise. A dog crate is a secure way to confine your dog for short periods during the day and to use as a comfortable bed at night. Crates come in wire mesh and in plastic. The wire ones are foldable to store flat in a smaller space. The plastic ones are more cozy, draft-free, and quiet, and are approved for airline travel.

Baby Gates: Since you shouldn't crate a dog for more than an hour or two at a time during the day, baby gates are a good way to limit your dog's freedom in the house. Be sure the baby gates you use are safe. The old-fashioned wooden, expanding lattice type has seriously injured a number of children by collapsing and trapping a leg, arm, or neck. That type of gate can hurt a puppy, too, so use the modern grid type gates instead. You'll need more than one baby gate if you have several doorways to close off.

Exercise Pen: Portable exercise pens are great when you have a young pup or a small dog. These metal or plastic pens are made of rectangular panels that are hinged together. The pens are freestanding, sturdy, foldable, and can be carried like a suitcase. You could set one up in your kitchen as the pup's daytime corral, and then take it outdoors to contain your pup while you garden or just sit and enjoy the day.

Enzymatic Cleaner: All dogs make housetraining mistakes. Accept this and be ready for it by buying an enzymatic cleaner made especially for pet accidents. Dogs like to eliminate where they have done it before, and lingering smells lead them to those spots. Ordinary household cleaners may remove all the odors you can smell, but only an enzymatic cleaner will remove everything your dog can smell.

The First Day

Housetraining is a matter of establishing good habits in your dog. That means you never want her to learn anything she will eventually have to unlearn. Start off housetraining on the right foot by teaching your dog that you prefer her to eliminate outside. Designate a potty area in your backyard (if you have one) or in the street in front of your home and take your dog to it as soon as you arrive home. Let her sniff a bit and, when she squats to go, give the action a name: "potty" or "do it" or anything else you won't be embarrassed to say in public. Eventually your dog will associate that word with the act and will eliminate on command. When she's finished, praise her with "good potty!"

That first day, take your puppy out to the potty area frequently. Although she may not eliminate every time, you are establishing a routine: You take her to her spot, ask her to eliminate, and praise her when she does.

Just before bedtime, take your dog to her potty area once more. Stand by and wait until she produces. Do not put your dog to bed for the night until she has eliminated. Be patient and calm. This is not the time to play with or excite your

Take your pup out frequently to her special potty spot and praise her when she goes.

dog. If she's too excited, a pup not only won't eliminate, she probably won't want to sleep either.

Most dogs, even young ones, will not soil their beds if they can avoid it. For this reason, a sleeping crate can be a tremendous help during housetraining. Being crated at night can help a dog develop the muscles that control elimination. So after your dog has emptied out, put her to bed in her crate.

A good place to put your dog's sleeping crate is near your own bed. Dogs are pack animals, so they feel safer sleeping with others in a common area. In your bedroom, the pup will be near you and you'll be close enough to hear when she wakes during the night and needs to eliminate.

Pups under 4 months old often are not able to hold their urine all night. If your puppy has settled down to sleep but awakens and fusses a few hours later, she probably needs to go out. For the best housetraining progress, take your pup to her elimination area whenever she needs to go, even in the wee hours of the morning.

Don't Overuse the Crate

A crate serves well as a dog's overnight bed, but you should not leave the dog in her crate for more than an hour or two during the day. Throughout the day, she needs to play and exercise. She is likely to want to drink some water and will undoubtedly eliminate. Confining your dog all day will give her no option but to soil her crate. This is not just unpleasant for you and the dog, but it reinforces bad cleanliness habits. And crating a pup for the whole day is abusive. Don't do it.

Your pup may soil in her crate if you ignore her late night urgency. It's unfair to let this happen, and it sends the wrong message about your expectations for cleanliness. Resign yourself to this midnight outing and just get up and take the pup out. Your pup will outgrow this need soon and will learn in the process that she can count on you, and you'll wake happily each morning to a clean dog.

The next morning, the very first order of business is to take your pup out to eliminate. Don't forget to take her to her special potty spot, ask her to eliminate, and then praise her when she does. After your pup empties out in the morning, give her breakfast, and then take her to her potty area again. After that, she shouldn't need to eliminate again

Your dog's crate is a great housetraining tool.

right away, so you can allow her some free playtime. Keep an eye on the pup though, because when she pauses in play she may need to go potty. Take her to the right spot, give the command, and praise if she produces.

Confine Your Pup

A pup or dog who has not finished housetraining should *never* be allowed the run of the house unattended. A new dog (especially a puppy) with unlimited access to your house will make her own choices about where to eliminate. Vigilance during your new dog's first few weeks in your home will pay big dividends. Every potty mistake delays housetraining progress; every success speeds it along.

Prevent problems by setting up a controlled environment for your new pet. A good place for a puppy corral is often the kitchen. Kitchens almost always have waterproof or easily cleaned floors, which is a distinct asset with leaky pups. A bathroom, laundry room, or enclosed porch could be used for a puppy corral, but the kitchen is generally the best location. Kitchens are a meeting place and a hub of activity for many families, and a puppy will learn better manners when she is socialized thoroughly with family, friends, and nice strangers.

The way you structure your pup's corral area is very important. Her bed, food, and water should be at the opposite end of the corral from the potty area. When you first get your pup, spread newspaper over the rest of the floor of her playpen corral. Lay the papers at least four pages thick and be sure to overlap the edges. As you note the pup's progress, you can remove the papers nearest the sleeping and eating corner. Gradually decrease the size of the papered area until only the end where you want the pup to eliminate is covered. If you will be training your dog to eliminate outside, place newspaper at the end of the corral that is closest to the door that leads outdoors. That way as she moves away from the clean area to the papered area, the pup will also form the habit of heading toward the door to go out.

Maintain a scent marker for the pup's potty area by reserving a small soiled piece of paper when you clean up. Place this piece, with her scent of urine, under the top sheet of the clean papers you spread. This will cue your pup where to eliminate.

Most dog owners use a combination of indoor papers and outdoor elimination areas. When the pup is left by herself in the corral, she can potty on the ever-present newspaper. When you are available to take the pup outside, she can do her business in the outdoor spot. It is not difficult to switch a pup from

Indoors, confine your pup in a corral with a bed and toys and a separate potty area that is away from where she plays and rests.

indoor paper training to outdoor elimination. Owners of large pups often switch early, but potty papers are still useful if the pup spends time in her indoor corral while you're away. Use the papers as long as your pup needs them. If you come home and they haven't been soiled, you are ahead.

When setting up your pup's outdoor yard, put the lounging area as far away as possible from the potty area, just as with the indoor corral setup. People with large yards, for example, might leave a patch unmowed at the edge of the lawn to serve as the dog's elimination area. Other dog owners teach the dog to relieve herself in a designated corner of a deck or patio. For an apartment-dwelling city dog, the outdoor potty area might be a tiny balcony or the curb. Each dog owner has somewhat different expectations for their dog. Teach your dog to eliminate in a spot that suits your environment and lifestyle.

> ### T I P
> #### Water
> Make sure your dog has access to clean water at all times. Limiting the amount of water a dog drinks is not necessary for housetraining success and can be very dangerous. A dog needs water to digest food, to maintain a proper body temperature and proper blood volume, and to clean her system of toxins and wastes. A healthy dog will automatically drink the right amount. Do not restrict water intake. Controlling your dog's access to water is not the key to housetraining her; controlling her access to everything else in your home is.

Be sure to pick up droppings in your yard at least once a day. Dogs have a natural desire to stay far away from their own excrement, and if too many piles litter the ground, your dog won't want to walk through it and will start eliminating elsewhere. Leave just one small piece of feces in the potty area to remind your dog where the right spot is located.

To help a pup adapt to the change from indoors to outdoors, take one of her potty papers outside to the new elimination area. Let the pup stand on the paper when she goes potty outdoors. Each day for four days, reduce the size of the paper by half. By the fifth day, the pup, having used a smaller and smaller piece of paper to stand on, will probably just go to that spot and eliminate.

Take your pup to her outdoor potty place frequently throughout the day. A puppy can hold her urine for only about as many hours as her age in months, and will move her bowels as many times a day as she eats. So a 2-month-old pup will urinate about every two hours, while at 4 months she can manage about four hours between piddles. Pups vary somewhat in their rate of development, so this is not a hard and fast rule. It does, however, present a realistic idea of how long a pup can be left without access to a potty place. Past 4 months, her potty trips will be less frequent.

Take your dog out frequently for regularly scheduled walks.

When you take the dog outdoors to her spot, keep her leashed so that she won't wander away. Stand quietly and let her sniff around in the designated area. If your pup starts to leave before she has eliminated, gently lead her back and remind her to go. If your pup sniffs at the spot, praise her calmly, say the command word, and just wait. If she produces, praise serenely, then give her time to sniff around a little more. She may not be finished, so give her time to go again before allowing her to play and explore her new home.

If you find yourself waiting more than five minutes for your dog to potty, take her back inside. Watch your pup carefully for twenty minutes, not giving her any opportunity to slip away to eliminate unnoticed. If you are too busy to watch the pup, put her in her crate. After twenty minutes, take her to the outdoor potty spot again and tell her what to do. If you're unsuccessful after five minutes, crate the dog again. Give her another chance to eliminate in fifteen or twenty minutes. Eventually, she will have to go.

Watch Your Pup

Be vigilant and don't let the pup make a mistake in the house. Each time you successfully anticipate elimination and take your pup to the potty spot, you'll move a step closer to your goal. Stay aware of your puppy's needs. If you ignore the pup, she will make mistakes and you'll be cleaning up more messes.

Keep a chart of your new dog's elimination behavior for the first three or four days. Jot down what times she eats, sleeps, and eliminates. After several days a pattern will emerge that can help you determine your pup's body rhythms. Most dogs tend to eliminate at fairly regular intervals. Once you know your new dog's natural rhythms, you'll be able to anticipate her needs and schedule appropriate potty outings.

Understanding the meanings of your dog's postures can also help you win the battle of the puddle. When your dog is getting ready to eliminate, she will display a specific set of postures. The sooner you can learn to read these signals, the cleaner your floor will stay.

A young puppy who feels the urge to eliminate may start to sniff the ground and walk in a circle. If the pup is very young, she may simply squat and go. All young puppies, male or female, squat to urinate. If you are housetraining a pup under 4 months of age, regardless of sex, watch for the beginnings of a squat as the signal to rush the pup to the potty area.

When a puppy is getting ready to defecate, she may run urgently back and forth or turn in a circle while sniffing or starting to squat. If defecation is imminent, the pup's anus may protrude or open slightly. When she starts to go, the pup will squat and hunch her back, her tail sticking straight out behind. There is no mistaking this posture; nothing else looks like this. If your pup takes this position, take her to her potty area. Hurry! You may have to carry her to get there in time.

A young puppy won't have much time between feeling the urge and actually eliminating, so you'll have to be quick to note her postural clues and intercept your pup in time. Pups from 3 to 6 months have a few seconds more between the urge and the act than younger ones do. The older your pup, the more time you'll have to get her to the potty area after she begins the posture signals that alert you to her need.

Accidents Happen

If you see your pup about to eliminate somewhere other than the designated area, interrupt her immediately. Say "wait, wait, wait!" or clap your hands loudly to startle her into stopping. Carry the pup, if she's still small enough, or take her collar and lead her to the correct area. Once your dog is in the potty area, give her the command to eliminate. Use a friendly voice for the command, then wait patiently for her to produce. The pup may be tense because you've just startled her and may have to relax a bit before she's able to eliminate. When she does her job, include the command word in the praise you give ("good potty").

The old-fashioned way of housetraining involved punishing a dog's mistakes even before she knew what she was supposed to do. Puppies were punished for breaking rules they didn't understand about functions they couldn't control. This was not fair. While your dog is new to housetraining, there is no need or excuse for punishing her mistakes. Your job is to take the dog to the potty area just before she needs to go, especially with pups under 3 months old. If you aren't watching your pup closely enough and she has an accident, don't punish the

It's not fair to expect a very young puppy to be able to control herself the way an adult dog can.

puppy for your failure to anticipate her needs. It's not the pup's fault; it's yours.

In any case, punishment is not an effective tool for housetraining most dogs. Many will react to punishment by hiding puddles and feces where you won't find them right away (like behind the couch or under the desk). This eventually may lead to punishment after the fact, which leads to more hiding, and so on.

Instead of punishing for mistakes, stay a step ahead of potty accidents by learning to anticipate your pup's needs. Accompany your dog to the designated potty area when she needs to go. Tell her what you want her to do and praise her when she goes. This will work wonders. Punishment won't be necessary if you are a good teacher.

What happens if you come upon a mess after the fact? Some trainers say a dog can't remember having eliminated, even a few moments after she has done so. This is not true. The fact is that urine and feces carry a dog's unique scent, which she (and every other dog) can instantly recognize. So, if you happen upon a potty mistake after the fact you can still use it to teach your dog.

But remember, no punishment! Spanking, hitting, shaking, or scaring a puppy for having a housetraining accident is confusing and counterproductive. Spend your energy instead on positive forms of teaching.

Take your pup and a paper towel to the mess. Point to the urine or feces and calmly tell your puppy, "no potty here." Then scoop or sop up the accident with the paper towel. Take the evidence and the pup to the approved potty area. Drop the mess on the ground and tell the dog, "good potty here," as if she had done the deed in the right place. If your pup sniffs at the evidence, praise her calmly. If the accident happened very recently your dog may not have to go yet, but wait with her a few minutes anyway. If she eliminates, praise her. Afterwards, go finish cleaning up the mess.

Soon the puppy will understand that there is a place where you are pleased about elimination and other places where you are not. Praising for elimination in the approved place will help your pup remember the rules.

Scheduling Basics

With a new puppy in the home, don't be surprised if your rising time is suddenly a little earlier than you've been accustomed to. Puppies have earned a reputation as very early risers. When your pup wakes you at the crack of dawn, you will have to get up and take her to her elimination spot. Be patient. When your dog is an adult, she may enjoy sleeping in as much as you do.

At the end of the chapter, you'll find a typical housetraining schedule for puppies aged 10 weeks to 6 months. (To find schedules for younger and older pups, and for adult dogs, visit this book's companion web site.) It's fine to adjust the rising times when using this schedule, but you should not adjust the intervals between feedings and potty outings unless your pup's behavior justifies a change. Your puppy can only meet your expectations in housetraining if you help her learn the rules.

The schedule for puppies is devised with the assumption that someone will be home most of the time with the pup. That would be the best scenario, of course, but is not always possible. You may be able to ease the problems of a latchkey pup by having a neighbor or friend look in on the pup at noon and take her to eliminate. A better solution might be hiring a pet sitter to drop by

Regular mealtimes will help you schedule predictable potty breaks for your dog.

midday. A professional pet sitter will be knowledgeable about companion animals and can give your pup high-quality care and socialization. Some can even help train your pup in both potty manners and basic obedience. Ask your veterinarian and your dog-owning friends to recommend a good pet sitter.

If you must leave your pup alone during her early housetraining period, be sure to cover the entire floor of her corral with thick layers of overlapping newspaper. If you come home to messes in the puppy corral, just clean them up. Be patient—she's still a baby.

Use this schedule (and the ones on the companion web site) as a basic plan to help prevent housetraining accidents. Meanwhile, use your own powers of observation to discover how to best modify the basic schedule to fit your dog's unique needs. Each dog is an individual and will have her own rhythms, and each dog is reliable at a different age.

Schedule for Pups 10 Weeks to 6 Months

7:00 a.m.	Get up and take the puppy from her sleeping crate to her potty spot.
7:15	Clean up last night's messes, if any.
7:30	Food and fresh water.
7:45	Pick up the food bowl. Take the pup to her potty spot; wait and praise.
8:00	The pup plays around your feet while you have your breakfast.
9:00	Potty break (younger pups may not be able to wait this long).
9:15	Play and obedience practice.
10:00	Potty break.
10:15	The puppy is in her corral with safe toys to chew and play with.
11:30	Potty break (younger pups may not be able to wait this long).
11:45	Food and fresh water.
12:00 p.m.	Pick up the food bowl and take the pup to her potty spot.
12:15	The puppy is in her corral with safe toys to chew and play with.

1:00	Potty break (younger pups may not be able to wait this long).
1:15	Put the pup on a leash and take her around the house with you.
3:30	Potty break (younger pups may not be able to wait this long).
3:45	Put the pup in her corral with safe toys and chews for solitary play and/or a nap.
4:45	Potty break.
5:00	Food and fresh water.
5:15	Potty break.
5:30	The pup may play nearby (either leashed or in her corral) while you prepare your evening meal.
7:00	Potty break.
7:15	Leashed or closely watched, the pup may play and socialize with family and visitors.
9:15	Potty break (younger pups may not be able to wait this long).
10:45	Last chance to potty.
11:00	Put the pup to bed in her crate for the night.

Appendix

Learning More About Your Pembroke Welsh Corgi

Some Good Books

About Corgis

EWING, SUE, *The Pembroke Welsh Corgi: Family Friend and Farmhand*, HOWELL BOOK HOUSE, 2000.

HARPER, DEBORAH S., *The New Complete Pembroke Welsh Corgi*, HOWELL BOOK HOUSE, 1994.

READ, CINDY, EDITOR, *Everything Corgi: Wit and Wisdom for Lovers of Cardis and Pems*, CORGIAID, 2002.

About Health Care

ELDREDGE, DEBRA M., DVM, AND LIISA D. CARLSON, DVM, DELBERT G., CARLSON, DVM, JAMES M. GIFFIN, MD, *Dog Owner's Home Veterinary Handbook*, 4TH EDITION, HOWELL BOOK HOUSE, 2007.

McCULLOUGH, SUSAN, *Senior Dogs For Dummies*, JOHN WILEY & SONS, 2004.

PITCAIRN, RICHARD, DVM, AND SUSAN HUBBLE PITCAIRN, *Dr. Pitcairn's Complete Guide to Natural Health for Dogs and Cats*, 3RD EDITION, RODALE BOOKS, 2005.

SHOJAI, AMY, *The First Aid Companion for Dogs & Cats*, RODALE BOOKS, 2001.

About Training

Benjamin, Carol Lea, *Surviving Your Dog's Adolescence*, Howell Book House, 1993.

Eldredge, Kate, and Debra M. Eldredge, *Head of the Class*, Howell Book House, 2006.

McConnell, Patricia, and Amy Moore, *Family Friendly Dog Training: A Six-Week Program for You and Your Dog*, Dog's Best Friend, 2007.

Volhard, Jack, and Wendy Volhard, *The Canine Good Citizen: Every Dog Can Be One*, 2nd edition, Howell Book House, 1997.

Dog Sports and Activities

Byron, Judy, and Adele Yunck, *Competition Obedience: A Balancing Act*, Jabby Productions, 1998.

Coile, Caroline D., *Silly Dog Tricks: Fun for You and Your Best Friend*, Sterling Publishing, 2006.

Kramer, Charles, *Rally-O: The Style of Rally Obedience*, 3rd edition, Fancee Publications, 2005.

Leach, Laurie, *The Beginner's Guide to Dog Agility*, TFH Publications, 2006.

DVD

An Introduction to All Breed Herding

Champion herding dog trainer Lynn Leach takes you to her Downriver Farm in British Columbia and shows you how to introduce your dog to herding, step by step. Order it at www.downriver.org.

Magazines

AKC Family Dog
P.O. Box 1964
Marion, OH 43306
www.akc.org/pubs/familydog

AKC Gazette
260 Madison Ave.
New York, NY 10016
www.akc.org/pubs/index.cfm

The Corgi Cryer
c/o Ms. Jeanne Gurnis
10 Jennifer Lane
Hartsdale, NY 10530-1219
www.mayflowercorgiclub.org/cryer

Dog Fancy
P.O. Box 37185
Boone, IA 50037-0185
www.dogfancy.com

Dog World
P.O. Box 37185
Boone, IA 50037-0185
www.dogworldmag.com

Dogs for Kids
P.O. Box 37184
Boone, IA 50037-0185
www.dogsforkids.com

Pembroke Welsh Corgi Newsletter
PWCCA
1130 Green Valley Rd.
Union Bridge, MD 21791
www.pwcca.org

Clubs and Registries

Pembroke Welsh Corgi Club of America
Anne Bowes
P.O. Box 2141
Duxbury, MA 02331-0110
www.pwcca.org
This is the national club for the breed; its web site has a great deal of information, including upcoming shows and competitions. There are also many all-
breed, individual breed, canine sport, and other special-interest dog clubs across
the country. The registries listed below can help you find clubs in your area.

American Kennel Club
260 Madison Ave.
New York, NY 10016
(212) 696-8200
www.akc.org

United Kennel Club
100 East Kilgore Rd.
Kalamazoo, MI 49002
(616) 343-9020
www.ukcdogs.com

Canadian Kennel Club
200 Ronson Dr.
Etobicoke, Ontario
Canada M9W 5Z9
(800) 250-8040 or (416) 675-5511
www.ckc.ca

Web Sites

All About Corgis

CorgiAid
www.corgiaid.org
This is the site of CorgiAid, a very active Corgi rescue organization.

Corgi-L Pembrokes
http://corgi-l.org/pembrokes
This site is organized and run by experienced Corgi fanciers. It includes lists of breeders and local breed clubs, and invaluable e-mail lists where you can learn about the breed.

Mayflower Pembroke Welsh Corgi Club
www.mayflowercorgiclub.org
This site of the Mayflower Pembroke Welsh Corgi Club contains a wealth of information, including referrals to breeders and rescue groups, Corgi care, and great Corgi gifts.

Dog Sports and Activities

The American Herding Breed Association
www.ahba-herding.org
This site has information regarding herding tests and trials for all herding breeds, including Corgis.

Canine Performance Events
www.k9cpe.com
This site is for the most user-friendly form of agility competition. It's open to all breeds.

Delta Society
www.deltasociety.org
The Delta Society promotes the human-animal bond through pet-assisted therapy and other programs.

Therapy Dogs International
www.tdi-dog.org
Therapy Dogs International provides information on the training and certification of therapy dogs.

World Canine Freestyle Organization
www.worldcaninefreestyle.org
This site is devoted to canine freestyle—dancing with your dog. There's information about freestyle events, tips, and even music.

Canine Health

American Animal Hospital Association
www.healthypet.com
If you want to check out veterinary hospitals in your area, the American Animal Hospital Association web site provides a database of AAHA-accredited veterinary hospitals. The site also provides information about vaccinations, pain management, and parasite protection.

American College of Veterinary Internal Medicine
www.acvim.org
This site includes a locator to help you find veterinarians and veterinary specialists in your area.

American Holistic Veterinary Medical Association
www.ahvma.org
If you're looking for a holistic veterinarian, the American Holistic Veterinary Medical Association has a database of veterinarians in your area. The site also provides information on holistic modalities.

American Veterinary Medical Association
www.avma.org
The American Veterinary Medical Association web site has a wealth of information for dog owners, from disaster preparedness to both common and rare diseases affecting canines. There is also information on choosing the right dog and dog bite prevention.

General Information

American Society for the Prevention of Cruelty to Animals
www.aspca.org
The ASPCA web site provides advice on pet care, animal behavior, disaster preparedness, and is a resource for poison-related animal emergencies.

DogWise
www.dogwise.com
A good site for books and DVDs on all aspects of dog ownership.

Infodog
www.infodog.com
This is a good site for locating AKC-licensed dog shows and obedience or agility trials in your area. It also links to rescue organizations nationwide.

Travel

Dog Friendly
www.dogfriendly.com
This web site publishes worldwide pet travel guides for dogs of all sizes and breeds. It includes information about dog-friendly events, attractions, resorts, vacation homes, and ski and beach locales throughout North America. Dog owners can benefit from the storm evacuation guide, tips on road trip preparation and travel etiquette, and even dog-friendly apartments.

Pets Welcome
www.petswelcome.com
Lists more than 25,000 hotels, B&Bs, ski resorts, campgrounds, and beaches that are pet-friendly. It even has listings you can download onto your GPS (global pooch system). The site supplies travel tips and blogs on travel recommendations for dog owners.

Index